W9-CPC-371

Special Districts

SPECIAL DISTRICTS

The Ultimate in Neighborhood Zoning

Richard F. Babcock
Wendy U. Larsen

Lincoln Institute of Land Policy
Cambridge, Massachusetts

The Lincoln Institute of Land Policy is a non-profit educational institution where leaders explore the complex linkages between public policies, including taxation, and land policy, and the impact of these linkages on major issues of our society. The Institute is a tax-exempt school providing advanced education in land economics, including property taxation, and offering challenging opportunities for learning, research, and publication.

Publication of a manuscript by the Lincoln Institute signifies that it is thought to be worthy of public consideration, but does not imply endorsement of conclusions, recommendations, or organizations that supported the research.

The Lincoln Institute is an equal opportunity institution in employment and admissions.

ISBN 1-55844-112-3

Library of Congress Cataloging-in-Publication Data

Babcock, Richard F.
    Special districts : the ultimate in neighborhood zoning / Richard F. Babcock, Wendy U. Larsen.
    187 p.   17.8 x 25.5 cm.
    ISBN 1-55844-112-3
    1. Zoning—New York (N.Y.)—History. 2. Zoning—California—San Francisco—History. 3. Zoning—Illinois—Chicago—History. 4. Special districts—New York (N.Y.)—History. 5. Special districts—California—San Francisco—History. 6. Special districts—Illinois—Chicago—History. I. Larsen, Wendy U. II. Title.
    HT169.73.N47B33   1990
    352.9'61'0973—dc20   90-45069
                           CIP

Cover design by Naomi Pierce.

Printed in the U.S.A. on acid-free text stock.

Lincoln Institute of Land Policy
Cambridge, Massachusetts

SE

To Marlin Smith,
our late revered partner,
who knew the perils of zoning litigation
and, better than most,
how to navigate successfully through them.

Contents

Foreword

America has had a good deal more experience destroying cities than building them. Many suspect the reasons for this may be buried deep in our cultural psyche, and so the trend will most likely persist. But, despite shameful neglect from our national government and the other overwhelming problems that cities face, there at least has been a positive change in the way we think and talk urban politics.

The movies no longer rely exclusively on the ritualized aerial view of the metropolis before zooming in to show frantic urbanites elbowing each other out of the way in pursuit of the rat race. Children's literature has by no means abandoned the unhappy caricature of the slick City Mouse, but there are more and more juvenile books set in cities and with unselfconscious portrayals of nonwhite families. Most significantly, television—through the good work of Sesame Street and Bill Cosby's sitcom—has at least succeeded in bringing the brownstone stoop into parity with Andy Hardy's front porch as a symbol of wholesome American life.

Among planners, there has been a palpable revival of interest in the physical city. This was born out of the need to deal with aroused communities opposed to unsympathetic change, out of frustration with the failure of more abstract policy pursuits, and, in many cases, out of long-held personal convictions. Now, the general ethos of the planning profession seems to be to enhance and extend existing patterns of settlement rather than to create new forms.

The tools at a city planner's disposal still need refining. In most American cities, or, for that matter, in most American small towns, the zoning in force is destructive—reflecting the largely suburban bias of the 1950s and a set of Corbusian spatial aspirations that have proved to be undesirable. The costs of revising these tools are daunting, the politics probably painful, and the rewards uncertain. It's a good time for Richard Babcock and Wendy Larsen's book.

There is a theory that the genius of a great city is not related to its gross dimensions but to the comprehensibility and strength of its distinctive parts. This idea is attractive in part because it provides a basis for decoding what would otherwise be a bewildering metropolis. It is unclear, however, whether planning tools could or should be tailored to reflect the effective distinctions between parts of a highly complex— i.e., urban—place.

A good spot to get a quick view of the intricacy of the urban problem is New York City's Little Italy. If you stand with your back against the serpentine wall of Old Saint Patrick's Cathedral and face the school where Chinese grade schoolers wear the green plaids of this once Irish parish, you can look left and right along Prince Street and see five or six quite different neighborhoods.

Looking west past Mulberry Street, where big Buicks with Jersey plates confirm the ominous presence of the Ravenite Social Club, over to busy Lafayette Street, you notice the scale change from tenements to chunky loft buildings. Further on is quiet Crosby Street with its unmoving trucks that serve the hidden factories above—factories where immigrant women huddle over sewing machines in conditions not much changed from those that shocked the country after the Triangle Shirtwaist fire.

Then comes Broadway, with its perpetual and exuberant Spanish bazaar where none of the merchandise seems remotely intended for the gallery goers, tourists, and resident artists who must weave through it all in order to enter the cooler, pricier precincts of SoHo. Beyond SoHo, the scale changes again in the South Village, where another Italian community dwindles in seeming harmony with a long-established middle-class overflow from Greenwich Village just to the north. A few blocks further, Prince Street ends at Sixth Avenue and so, too, does the city's nineteenth century character, which begins to give way there to more modern buildings that house businesses relating to trucking and print-

ing—now in the process of being displaced by the northward
growth of the financial district.

Glancing east past Mott Street, you see a seemingly
equal mix of young Hispanics, younger (than SoHo) artists,
and residual Italians patronizing an early Original Ray's
Pizza. One block over, Elizabeth Street—just recently re-
stored by Hollywood for the latest Godfather sequel—serves
by night as an apparently unassailable retail outlet for
Columbian drug dealers. A block beyond that, our perspective
is closed by the solid wall of the Bowery, home to endless
lamp shades, great slag heaps of used restaurant stoves, and,
of course, a vast army of homeless men—many of whom will
end their lives in one of the horrific private hotels or charita-
ble shelters that line the street. From end to end, from the
depths of despair and brutality to the heights of artistic and
commercial success with a lot of distinctive territory in between, Prince Street is only four-fifths of a mile long.

The mind boggles at the thought of comprehending, let
alone trying to control, this level of complexity across the
city. Yet here and elsewhere, a beginning has been made.
Along Prince Street alone, Little Italy, SoHo (including
Broadway), and the Bowery are all subject to special zoning,
historic, or urban renewal districts.

How well these work and to what ends has been, until
now, a largely unexamined subject. Even harder to know is
what forces will compel change in the future. New waves of
immigrants are arriving in unprecedented numbers. By 1992,
for the first time since the beginning of this century, over half
of New York's population will have been born outside the
country. These new New Yorkers, like those before them, will
bring terrible problems and wonderful opportunities. Rapidly
changing political and economic alignments in Europe may
affect the inflow of capital, just as improved telecommunica-
tions, worsening race relations, and disadvantageous tax
rates might reaccelerate the now-slowed exodus of corporate
employers. With so many unknowns and so much outside our
control, it may seem frivolous to be troubling over the efficacy
of special district zoning tools. As the old line goes, isn't it like
rearranging the deck chairs on the *Titanic*?

Well, of course, it might be. Cities can disappear cataclysmically (in fact, the Nazis had targeted a spot just south of Prince Street as ground zero for an atomic attack), but happily it is more often the case that cities grow and decline incrementally. Special districts have been hailed as a highly effective approach to accommodating incremental growth in ways that strengthen sound neighborhoods and buffer weaker ones. In my view, Richard Babcock and Wendy Larsen are wasting neither their time nor ours in providing this pioneering and provocative analysis of how things have actually worked out. They have approached this task with a cold eye for facts and a warm heart for intent, which seems an appropriate ambivalence for celebrated zoning lawyers who clearly harbor an inexplicable and probably incurable affection for urban life.

The approach to New York, San Francisco, and Chicago is anecdotal, which gives the authors license to have a little fun characterizing the principal political, community, and planning players without coming down too hard on one side or another. It will certainly assure the sort of spirited response the issue deserves, and, one suspects, the authors relish. Ultimately, the implicit question is not resolved, leading me to conclude that the book's hidden agenda is nothing less than to pick a very good fight. Or better yet, a series.

Kent Barwick
President
The Municipal Art Society of New York
New York City
July, 1990

Acknowledgements

We want to thank the many people who patiently, and often repeatedly, put up with our interviews and telephone calls, in particular: Sandy Hornick, Norman Marcus, Kent Barwick, Richard Satkin, Virginia Waters, William Ryan, and Conn Howe in New York City; Robin Jones and Inge Horton in San Francisco; and Charlie Siemon and Gregory Longhini in Chicago.

We are also indebted to the numerous people who frequently, often anonymously, sent us news clippings, articles, and other material that recounted, insightfully, incidents that were of help.

We are also grateful to Frank Schnidman, who sponsored the idea initially, to the Lincoln Institute of Land Policy for its generous backing, and especially to Anne Brophy, our editor, who displayed a degree of patience and understanding above and beyond that which we ever expected.

But above all, only we are responsible for the contents of this work, and we apologize in advance for any errors that may be found herein.

Dick Babcock
Wendy Larsen
Chicago, Illinois
September 1990

Prologue

> *What happened to special zoning districts was a lit-*
> *tle like what happened to penicillin. When penicillin*
> *was first introduced, it acquired a reputation as a*
> *'miracle drug' and was prescribed in many situa-*
> *tions for which it was not appropriate.*
>
> Jonathan Barnett
> *An Introduction to Urban Design, 1982*

Background

Planning and zoning, as with so much else in American society, went through a radical period in the 1960s and early 1970s. "Advocacy planning" became a rallying cry for professional planners who confronted the politics and judgments of City Hall with pontifical recipes for a new generation of "cities beautiful." Neighborhood planning—organized (or disorganized) public planning—was another idea whose time seemed to have come, particularly in larger cities. Trial by neighborism and other art forms of citizen activism ascended to new heights. More of anything new—planners and decision-making bodies, plans and regulations—seemed to be the rule, one land-use fad after another.

Since the mid-1970s, the bloom has left the flower; we have become more conservative and cautious. In many places, City Hall has simply waited out the shouts and curses of the locals and then gone back to business as usual. In other cities, zoning has become worse than it was before: more complex and sophisticated, yet less efficient and fair.

Bargaining for zoning—the "let's make a deal" mentality —and the resulting uncertainty about the rules became the

common denominator of zoning in the 1980s. A new and in-
sidious dimension was added to the already frustrating permitting game—exactions, otherwise known as legalized ex-
tortion. Exactions expanded exponentially, driven by
increasing fiscal distress within local government and a deal-
making generation. Cynical observers suggested that the
system of bargains and exactions was little more than "zoning for sale." Zoning grants that had originally been free
were now for sale at a price that was negotiated during an
often lengthy bargaining process. Cities demanded more and
more cash from developers, and the latter, taking out their
pencils and figuring the costs and time involved in litigation,
more often than not paid the asking price in order to receive
their approvals without delay. For the most part, exactions
seem to have done little for the quality of land-use decisions
except to make the development process more expensive.

Partly in response to these and other abuses of zoning,
many critics have written learned expositions on why zoning
should be abolished—what one author described as "bemoaning zoning."[1] But others know that such an idea cannot be sold
to elected officials and their constituents who believe that the
ability of zoning to protect the status quo is the be-all and end-
all of life in the city. Zoning is a mainstream component of city
politics and power, and, like it or not, it is here to stay.

A few states, in response to some of the more dubious local zoning practices, have reconsidered the traditional view
that states should leave zoning power and reform strictly in
the hands of local government. In the 1980s, Hawaii, Florida,
Oregon, California, and Vermont passed laws to inject the
state into at least major land-use decisions, usually through
planning requirements. New York, Minnesota, and New Jersey approached reform on a regional basis, respectively creating the Adirondacks Park Agency, the Minneapolis–St.
Paul Metro Council, the Hackensack Meadowlands Development Commission, and the Pinelands Commission. The vast
majority of states, however, have been content to cope with
zoning enabling acts that, with only an occasional later
amendment, date back to the time of the Standard State

Zoning Enabling Act, first published in 1922 and adopted by many states soon afterward.

Through it all, uniformity, one of the fundamental principles of zoning when the concept was "blessed" by the United States Supreme Court in *Village of Euclid v. Ambler Realty Corp.*,[2] has taken a beating. More and more, the response to a particular localized problem has been a particular "fix" without regard to uniformity, comprehensiveness, or any of the other theoretical principles of sound planning and plan implementation. The formula is simple: if a problem crops up in one neighborhood, forget about the organic issues that caused the problem, forget about comprehensive planning, forget about the "forest," and, instead, ease the political pressures from unhappy neighbors with a quick and narrowly tailored "solution" that avoids comprehensive planning—simply focus on the "trees."

The Special District Phenomenon

This book is the story of a zoning phenomenon that has arisen in this complex and volatile environment as a perceived antidote or "cure" for "neighborhood" problems: the "special district." This concept has reached its apogee or nadir, depending on your perspective, in New York City and San Francisco but is also used in many cities throughout the country. The "special district" we are discussing in this book is an amendment to the text of a zoning ordinance creating a new zoning district with regulations that are tailor-made to some particular set of circumstances in a particular area. Special districts are, at least in part, a result of the susceptibility and hostility of neighborhoods to change. Although often an outgrowth or result of neighborhood planning, they generally focus on preserving the status quo.

Some observers see nothing remarkable about special districts. They point to planned unit development districts (PUDs) and historic districts as more familiar examples of discrete regulatory districts targeted to a limited number of parcels. Special districts are not the same, however, as these

more traditional zoning techniques. PUDs are usually created for undeveloped areas, not established neighborhoods.
Moreover, special districts often serve and embrace a broader
range of problems than do traditional historic preservation
districts. Indeed, there may be no architectural or historic
significance to an area protected by a special district; city fa-
thers and mothers may have concluded for purely political or
economic reasons that it was necessary to have a special zoning treatment for a particular area.

> Special district zoning...represents a significant depar-
> ture from this traditional Euclidian zoning concept
> ....The districts created are not traditional zoning dis-
> tricts, narrowly limited to particular uses, but broad-
> based plans intended to preserve and enhance troubled
> areas of the City which, because of their singular charac-
> teristics, are important to its wealth and vitality.[3]

Rather than being similar to traditional zoning techniques,
the special district is more akin to such new ideas as the
"specific plan" developed in California and Arizona, a technique that carries the concept of special treatment to a logical extreme.

Sometimes, perhaps more often than not, the special
district technique is "dispensed" with little or no forethought
—usually nothing more than the minimum needed to satisfy
the politics of the situation. Other times, special districts are
the result of exhaustive planning exercises and very intense
(some would say too much) citizen activism. These extremes
in special district planning reflect how much City Hall
thought it could get away with—politically and legally—in
each particular situation. We do not mean to imply that
there is no forethought behind the creation of a special district. All of the special districts we studied originated with
someone's vision of a thing he or she wanted to protect from
a perceived threat, though many of the visions were extremely parochial and all too often based on an exaggerated
value placed on the things that people were trying to protect.

The special district is appealing and very seductive—at
least from the political perspective. The concept may have
less appeal to the administrator faced with enforcing what

are, in effect, separate zoning ordinances. The technique is, by all accounts, an effective means of protecting a particular area from development pressure or of preserving the appearance of a grand boulevard that is threatened by change. For example, New York's Special Fifth Avenue District is undoubtedly good at preserving an ambience that is known around the world. But, as we shall see, special districts have problems that should be considered by any city contemplating their use. Some of these problems call into question whether special districts represent a step forward or, as some argue, two steps backward.

New York, San Francisco, and Chicago: Voices of Experience

Whether or not the City of New York is, in fact, the originator, it is the undisputed monarch of special district use with thirty-seven separate special districts. (For brief descriptions, see Appendix A.) Much of this book, therefore, examines the New York experience, one that is both rich and spicy. New York is a particularly useful focus because the City has encountered the full range of problems and possibilities of special districts.

We also draw on the experience of San Francisco and Chicago to show that the technique need not be and has not been confined to the largest metropolis in the country. In our opinion, there are common threads of the special district concept wherever it is found. We believe that the seductive siren of expedient political solutions will continue to make the concept enticing to municipalities wherever neighborhoods are faced with unpopular change and comprehensive solutions are too expensive, time-consuming, and politically disruptive.

Purpose and Methodology

Special districts continue to grow in popularity across the country. Our purpose in this book is to illuminate the problems and benefits associated with special districts for those who are considering using the technique in their own cities. Using case studies of individual special districts in New York and other cities, we will identify the wide range of techniques they employ to accomplish a variety of purposes. We will ask how the effects of special districts compare with their purposes in order to evaluate their success as an alternative to comprehensive zoning revision or targeted regulatory districts.

This is a book about the politics, debates, and opinions that accompany the special district phenomenon—the true heart of the zoning process. To understand these issues, we collected much of our information from numerous interviews (see Appendix E), as well as the ordinances themselves and other printed materials. This is *not* a book for planners who are interested in all the technical minutiae of numbers, plans, and ordinances; we leave those details for future authors. This book is for all those who enjoy a good story about the fascinating world of land-use law and politics.

Before we can embark on an exploration of individual special districts, the reader needs to have a basic understanding of the players in this particular version of the "Zoning Game." While New York City's political climate and institutions are somewhat unique in the nether world of big city politics, an understanding of their dynamics is helpful (and interesting) for anyone trying to appreciate the special district phenomenon. Chapter 2 describes the main players in New York City; a series of case studies begins with Chapter 3.

The Players

The Land-Use Game
in New York City

Nobody believes the Plan Commission anymore.
New York Zoning Attorney

Special zoning districts do not occur in a vacuum. They are perhaps the most political creations of the very politicized process known as urban zoning. Every level of a city's political structure, from neighborhood groups to the mayor, gets involved. The differing agendas of these various players have a profound influence on how special districts are created and administered. One of the major problems with New York's special districts is that the idea was dreamed up by one administration but largely implemented by another.

New York City Government:
Pre-1990

Major changes in the structure of New York City's government occurred in late 1989. Because special districts were shaped under the city's original political system, it is necessary to take some time to describe it. We will conclude this chapter with a description of the radically new government structure that began operation in January, 1990.

Ever since the five boroughs (Manhattan, Brooklyn, Queens, Bronx, and Staten Island) were merged by the state

legislature in 1897, the City of New York was governed by a
rather unusual political system. The Mayor was—and still
is—the Chief Executive Officer (CEO). Opposite the Mayor,
the Board of Estimate sat at the top of the city's legislative
structure. Among its other powers, the Board controlled land
use, contracts, and franchise, and it participated in the approval of the budget. The Board consisted of eight members,
three of whom—the Mayor, the City Comptroller, and the
President of the City Council—were elected at large and had
two votes each on all matters. The other five members were
the presidents of the five boroughs and had one vote apiece.

The City Council—in most cities the real legislative
power—was relatively powerless; as one commentator put it,
"the Council does little except name streets." The Board of
Standards and Appeals played the role of the customary
Board of Zoning Appeals and approved variances.

At the neighborhood level, there were—and still are—the
Community Boards. Created in 1975 by an amendment to the
City's charter, the fifty-nine Community Boards throughout
the City each consist of up to fifty unsalaried members appointed by the Borough President. Each member must reside
or have an interest (work or own property) in the neighborhood. The City provides these Boards with nominal funds suf-
ficient to hire an executive director, who directs the small
staff and generally acts as an ombudsman for the community.
Board actions are basically advisory. The Boards call public
meetings on the budget, land-use matters, and other major issues. Any zoning changes that might result from a special
permit or a variance must come before the Board, whose opinion must be considered by the city-wide agency that makes
the final decision. Needless to say, there are wide divergences
among the Boards in their interest in community affairs and
the pressure they bring to bear on the Board of Estimate, the
Mayor, and the Board of Standards and Appeals.

Prior to 1990, the five-member Planning Commission,
first created by charter in 1936, was appointed by the Mayor
with the approval of the Board of Estimate. The Mayor designated one Commission member as chairperson. The Commission, in turn, appointed its large staff and executive di-

rector. In addition to the main office, the Planning Commission had branch offices in each of the five boroughs. When the Commission identified a particularly important problem, it could name staff members to serve as a "group" to work on solving the problem. Two examples of important and influential "groups" were the Urban Design Group of distinguished urban designers that first introduced the special district concept to New York in the late 1960s, and the more recent Zoning Study Group under the direction of Sandy Hornick. The Commission was generally held in high respect in the City, at least until the last years of the Koch administration. With very few exceptions, its chairperson was a powerful figure.

The Mayor and the Planning Commission*

It should not be surprising that the attitude of the chief executive of a city will be reflected in the quality of and positions taken by his subordinates. They are his people. New York City's experience will show that special districts seem to be most successful and least abused when the Mayor has an interest in and commitment to planning.

When John Lindsay was elected Mayor in 1966, he brought with him what we can only call his WASPish vision of a glorious urbanscape. He created a Planning Commission that shared those values. Among other things, he hired and encouraged the Urban Design Group—the so-called "red brigade" of urban designers, all dispersed now—that was meant to create an Oz on the banks of the Hudson. It was these urban designers who originated special districts in New York City. The result of Lindsay's reign was the brink of bankruptcy, transit strikes, and uncollected garbage.

*Most of this chapter focuses on the Koch administration, which, by virtue of its long duration, had the greatest impact on the City's special districts. Because our research was completed before David Dinkins was sworn in as Mayor and before the revised charter had gone into effect, we will confine our discussion of the Dinkins administration to predictions about the likely effects of these changes.

His successor, Mayor Abraham Beame (1974-78), did not do much to change things. Cautious and uninspired, he was generally satisfied to let things coast along.

Mayor Ed Koch (1978-90) was a different breed of cat. Wisecracking, offensive to blacks, and insufferably righteous, this former Congressman from Greenwich Village knew little about city planning and cared less. His principal concern was to get the City back on its feet financially following the near disaster of the mid-seventies. And this he did pretty well, overseeing New York's move from a negative cash flow to a dollar surplus. He also suffered in his third term from an embarrassment of corruption, none of which directly touched him.

The way in which Koch accomplished the City's return to fiscal health is the matter that concerns us. Raising new revenue to ease the City's fiscal crisis clearly became a primary concern. As we shall detail below, Koch's City behaved like an entrepreneur, a moneymaking machine, rather than like an urban planner.

This should not come as a shock. When Koch took office, the City was a near shambles and had reached that state under a mayor who fervently believed in planning. The general consensus is that Koch was indifferent to planning. Neither was he really interested in the concept of special districts, except as the movers and shakers (e.g., the Midtown district) might pressure him or important political allies might demand one (e.g., the garment district). A reflection of his attitude may be the current opinion of the Planning Commission staff that special districts have been carried too far (we will discuss this attitude in more detail in Chapter 8).

One of the planners who was on staff when Lindsay was in office described to us the difference between Lindsay's and Koch's attitudes about planning:

> I was there in the heyday. It was the last optimistic period of planning in New York....It was a very closeknit group of people anyway who were doing all of this. It was a time when we, staff and City Planning, had a very direct connection to the Mayor's office, certainly under Lindsay and even under Beame. Under Koch, I don't

think he even cares; other than wanting to get the development done, he hasn't got the foggiest idea about zoning, doesn't care about physical planning. But under Lindsay and Beame, urban design, planning, and zoning were a major concern of the Mayor's office....So that was all very close and tight, and then Koch had virtually no interest in it. I think that is part of the demoralization [in the Planning Commission now] because there is just political pressure to get stuff done. Just get this thing out; let's move it along. We're fueling the economy here, and, in a way, there is still a depression mentality, that we're still in the middle 1970s, which I think is also really not true.

Another former member of the Lindsay Urban Design Group was a wee bit more optimistic about the role of the Planning Commission under Koch:

Beame was so conservative that he didn't change anything. So the [planning] apparatus stayed in place all during Beame's administration. It's Koch who has dismantled it because I think he feels it gets in the way of developers. But even Koch has not been able to dismantle it as much as he would like to because there is now a very strong planning constituency which probably wasn't there twenty-five years ago.

Under Koch, the Planning Commission was out of the mainstream of current political power. As a consequence, there was a diminished morale among the staff. One planner now involved with a private housing watchdog group put it most bluntly: "I personally think that Koch is the worst thing that has ever happened to the City....I believe that, under Koch, basic, fundamental, decision-making powers over land use, development, housing, have been taken out of the public's hands and given to the private sector. So not only is he not interested in it [planning], I think he's actively hostile to it." According to another ex-Lindsay aide: "I don't think Ed Koch really believes in planning."

Koch and Developers

New York City today probably is much more alive economically than it was thirteen years ago. One has only to walk through Midtown Manhattan to see the changes.

Urban planning advocates point out that this economic growth has had a price. New buildings, such as the AT&T headquarters and IBM Center, were squeezed into cramped spaces using every zoning bonus the City could give to them. One of the most-used bonuses was the provision of the 1961 comprehensive zoning amendment that provided extra floor area ratio (FAR) for constructing urban plazas. The result was a proliferation of cold and forbidding plazas everywhere in mid-Manhattan, as William Whyte demonstrated in his book *The Social Life of Small Urban Spaces* (Conservation Foundation, 1986) and in his short film of the same title. Midtown Manhattan has become the Golden Goose that some say is now in danger of being strangled by those who would profit from it. While the rezoning of Midtown in 1982 (see Chapter 6) has relieved the development pressure on Midtown to some extent, it has exacerbated the problem in nearby Clinton (see Chapter 4).

The reader will be surprised to learn that, for all of Koch's devotion to development, he was not popular with developers. That is the sentiment we heard in numerous off-the-record conversations with builders. One reason that Koch was unpopular is the real estate tax system; the other—ironically—is New York State's Environmental Protection Act. As neither law can be blamed on Koch's administration, we are sure that the negative attitude of developers must have puzzled him.

The real estate tax system in New York would shock a visitor from Los Angeles or Chicago. Property taxes on commercial buildings are astronomically higher in New York than in other cities. A building in New York that sells for $300 per square foot will, in a few years, wind up with an annual tax bill of $16 per square foot. In Los Angeles, a building that sells for $350 per square foot will have taxes of $3 per square foot. One knowledgeable real estate developer told us in 1988:

> And the growth-class buildings here are not more valuable than the world-class buildings in other places according to the Japanese investors who are buying in both cities. They're spending between $300 and $400 per square foot on buildings in Los Angeles, Chicago, Boston, Washington, New York....If you bought these buildings in these five cities for $300-$400 per square foot, which is the sort of fancy office building price, the taxes in New York would wind up being double what they would be in Chicago, three and a half times what they would be in Boston and Washington, and eight times what they would be in Los Angeles.

Office buildings labor under these heavy taxes in part because of the tax subsidy given to homeowners in the five boroughs. One resident told us that he had a brownstone in Brooklyn on which he paid $1,700 in property taxes in 1988. "It allows us," he added, "to send our kids to private schools because the city schools don't work." The city also lost income from residential buildings in part because of the rent control that had been in existence long before Koch took office. In New York, residential landlords can successfully block a raise in taxes if the raise exceeds the legally permitted limit for rent increases.

New York State's Environmental Protection Act must also be factored into the equation. Any new building proposal can expect a challenge that the environmental impact statement (EIS) was inadequate; most proposals do get challenged. Preparing such statements—and fighting them—has become a big industry. John E. Zuccotti, CEO of a large real estate corporation, former Chairman of the Planning Commission (1973-75), former Deputy Mayor (1976-78), and a very successful lawyer for developers, told us:

> It's really the environmental process that holds you up because it's a never-ending process. It's mush. If you think planning is mush, the environmental stuff is really mush...I could be finished with a complex project from start to finish, compromising all the thorny planning

questions in eighteen months. Now it's more like three
years...every major case is an invitation to a lawsuit. Every single major project that I work on today has resulted in a lawsuit....We get them from legal service
groups, from community groups, and from competitors
who are trying to stop the project.

The state environmental protection law itself may not, of
course, be blamed on Koch. But its existence, plus the tax situation, may explain why Koch, for all his pro-development
posture, was not all that popular with developers. The City's
greed does not necessarily ensure the affection of those who
benefit from that municipal avidity—which must have per-
plexed the Koch administration.

The City v. the Citizenry:
the Coliseum Site

Not surprisingly, the City's development activities during the Koch administration occasionally came into conflict
with the interests of its citizens, as represented by the Community Boards and groups such as the Municipal Art Society.
One of the most extreme examples of the City's craving for
money at the public's expense resulted in a fight which illustrates the dynamics between City government and citizen organizations, and points out the importance of the Mayor's attitude toward planning in how planning decisions are made.
New York City probably owns over 13,000 parcels of
land in the five boroughs, obtained through tax forfeiture or
acquisitions that were not developed. By all accounts, the
Koch administration was determined to sell many of these
parcels and to get the best price for them the market would
bring. One of the City's most recent and outrageous deals
concerned the disposition of the old Coliseum site at Columbus Circle.** By the time it was concluded, the deal had pre-

---

**Much of what follows is adapted from a portion of Richard Bab-
cock's article "The City as Entrepreneur: Fiscal Wisdom or Regulatory
Folly?" that will be included in the book on *City Deal Making*, to be published by The Urban Land Institute, summer, 1990.

cipitated a major dispute between the City of New York and a group led by the Municipal Art Society.

The Coliseum site, three and a half acres on the west side of Columbus Circle close to the southwest corner of Central Park, was acquired by the City and the Metropolitan Transport Authority in 1953 for $2.1 million. At that time, it had an FAR of 6.7. When the Javits Convention Center was planned for another site in the early 1980s, it became apparent that the Coliseum site was obsolete. In 1982, the Koch administration decided to dispose of the parcel and put out a Request for Proposal (RFP). The principal criteria for selection of the winning proposal were, to put it mildly, blunt:

1. The amount of the purchase price offered, which will be the primary consideration;
2. The economic viability of the proposal...; and
3. The overall benefit of the proposal to the City....The Sponsor intends to sell the Site to the applicant whose proposal most successfully meets the Sponsor's goals, *particularly the goal of realizing the highest financial return from the sale.*[1] (emphasis added)

The RFP also required the bidders to apply for a bonus of 20 percent of floor area ratio in return for spending money to refurbish the IRT, a subway station at Columbus Circle, and build a new connection to it.

When the bids came in, the most attractive one (although not the highest) was from Boston Properties, which offered $455 million. Boston Properties was joined by Salomon Brothers, the brokerage house, which was to be the major tenant. The principal owner of Boston Properties is Mortimer B. Zuckerman, a real estate developer and a magazine owner from Boston, who had been embroiled in controversy before. He precipitated a major battle in Boston when he proposed a Park Plaza Hotel next to the Boston Common that threatened to cast a shadow far across the Common. In August, 1987, he announced plans to build an office park near Walden Pond in Concord, Massachusetts, which still has local conservationists in an uproar.

When the City announced the deal in February, 1987, a most unusual provision of the agreement was also disclosed.

Boston Properties would, of course, apply for a bonus to the City Planning Commission and the Board of Estimate (and agree to spend $40 million on subway improvements), but if Zuckerman did *not* get the bonus, New York City would give him back $57 million! When Boston Properties applied, it got its bonus....Surprise!

The rest of the City permitting process was equally smooth. The Board of Estimate voted 10-1 in favor of the proposal. (Koch's Planning Commission had already stamped its approval.) The lone dissenter, according to Sydney Schanberg, columnist for *Newsday*, was David Dinkins, then the President of the Borough of Manhattan. Schanberg reported that "Dinkins was the only member of the Board of Estimate to deem the issue important enough to appear in person. All the others sent surrogates to occupy their chairs, by that act affirming that the conclusion, as the cliche goes, was foregone."[2]

When the design concept was disclosed, outrage was the reaction: the project had twin towers of sixty-eight and fifty-eight stories, 2.3 million square feet of floor area, 350 luxury condominiums at the top, enough office space for 8,000 or more workers, a five-story indoor retail mall, and ten movie theaters. As Schanberg reported in *Newsday* on February 2, 1987: "Just the bonus floor space alone—450,000 square feet—is two-thirds the size of the largest building in the Columbus Circle vicinity, the forty-three story Gulf and Western Building."[3]

The three Community Boards in the area formed a coalition to oppose it. Paul Goldberger, architecture critic for the *New York Times*, not only had repeated conniptions over the proposed building's appearance and bulk but also criticized the City's role in the development process. He wrote:

> So not only had the city decided to sell off a corner of the park for cash; it had not even cared enough to guarantee good architecture in the bargain. It is the city that is the real villain of this tale, for the same indifference to any deeper values on the part of the city government that led to its failure to set strong design guidelines for Columbus Center was evident in the project's very conception.

There was a complete confusion of roles at Columbus Center, a confusion that is really rather horrifying in its implications. Real estate developers are not supposed to be the guardians of the public trust; they are supposed to make money. The city government, through its zoning power, is supposed to act as a check on the zeal of the private sector, as a protector of the public interest. When Boston Properties bid $455.1 million for the Coliseum site, it was simply doing what it was supposed to do, and was playing by the rules. It was the city that had set those rules, and turned the development process into something resembling a land rush. Had the City decided, instead, that a smaller building would be in the public interest, and set a ceiling on bids and established meaningful design guidelines, the result would have been altogether different.[4]

Kent Barwick, President of the Municipal Art Society, agreed in placing most of the blame upon the City: "I'm not nominating Mort [Zuckerman] for man of the year, but at least he's a developer who is behaving like a developer....Our complaint is that the City is a government that's behaving like a developer."

With a flair reminiscent of its performance during the battle over saving Grand Central Station, the Municipal Art Society lined up a gaggle of prominent figures to protest the proposal, including Henry Kissinger and Bill Moyers (who testified before the Board of Estimate). Even Zuckerman acknowledged the effectiveness of this strategy to the *New York Times*: "No developer wants to go up against the likes of Jackie Onassis and Paul Newman and Norman Lear....No matter what the facts are, a developer will never be perceived as a victim or a sympathetic figure."[5] In a display of *étulage* redolent of its Preservation Whistle Stop Train to Washington two days preceding oral arguments before the United States Supreme Court in the Grand Central case, the Society, on Sunday, October 18, 1987, brought out more than 800 people to Central Park South to form a slanting line from Columbus Circle to Fifth Avenue. When a signal was given at 1:30 p.m., the protesters opened their umbrellas one after another to demonstrate the shadow the building would cause.

The Society did more. Joined by the Metropolitan Chapter of the American Planning Association and the New York Parks Council, it filed suit against the City of New York, the Board of Estimate of the City of New York, Edward I. Koch, individually and as Mayor of the City of New York, the City Planning Commission (CPC) of the City of New York, the Metropolitan Transportation Authority, and the Triborough Bridge and Tunnel Authority (TBTA). The plaintiffs sought to annul the actions of respondents authorizing the sale. They pointed out, as had the local press, that the proceeds from the sale had already been included in the City's 1988 budget. The City and the Metropolitan Transportation Authority had agreed to split the money from the sale evenly.

The plaintiffs' first charge was that the "bid requirements amounted to a sale of a zoning bonus." Because this was New York City (where an EIS is required by state law), they also charged that there was inadequate environmental analysis of traffic, light, and pollution.

On December 7, 1987, Judge Edward H. Lehner handed down his opinion. Noting that "in return for the grant by the CPC of the 20 percent floor area ratio bonus, the City is obtaining not only $35 to $40 million of local subway improvements, but an additional $57 million in cash to be employed for other purposes," Lehner concluded: "A proper *quid pro quo* for the grant of the right to increase the bulk of a building may not be the payment of additional cash into the City's coffers for citywide use....In conclusion, the court finds that the contract with the developer provides for an illegal payment. Consequently, the approvals thereof by the City and TBTA are null and void."[6]

The Society was jubilant. Koch was apoplectic. After suggesting that the people who opposed it—whom he dubbed "the parasol set" for their umbrella stunt—probably never rode the subway that would have benefitted from the deal, he barked: "There will be fewer policemen, fewer sanitation workers, fewer teachers and substantially fewer dollars for transit....Thousands of municipal jobs would be at risk."[7]

What would the City do? What would Zuckerman do? Tough questions. Salomon Brothers had pulled out of the project after the crash in October, 1987. Zuckerman agreed to scale down the building by 16 percent and give back the bonus. Boston Properties hired a new architect, who submitted a design for a smaller building more in keeping with its context. The City proposed that Zuckerman get a reduction of up to $75 million on his purchase price and freed him from his $40 million obligation to fix up the subway at Columbus Circle. In addition, the City gave Zuckerman $50 million in tax concessions and $15 million relief on interest payments. Newspapers reported that fourteen other developers who had originally submitted bids wanted the City to reopen all the bids. Too much delay, said the City. Critics such as Paul Goldberger applauded the new design but were still unhappy with the large bulk of the building, arguing that it was still too large for the site.[8]

When we asked an assistant corporation counsel in July, 1988, he insisted that the City would appeal Judge Lehner's decision. Kent Barwick scoffed at this and said that a Notice of Appeal (filed by the City) was just a "publicity ploy." Yet, in August, 1988, the City did file a brief on appeal. At the beginning of the brief, the City's reasons for pursuing the case were stated frankly:

> The extraordinary result below touches on an issue of vital public importance. Unless it is reversed, it is likely to thwart or cast doubt on the legality of similar future transactions in property owned by any governmental entity in the State of New York.[9]

There was a question about whether or not there was anything left to appeal. Salomon was gone; the building had been changed. Would not the case be moot? In fact, after a third and yet smaller plan was submitted by the developer, the City and its opponents agreed to dismiss the appeal.

Where was the Planning Commission during all of this? Given the climate of the Koch administration, it is not surprising that the Planning Commission played second fiddle, doing little more than rubber-stamping the Mayor's deals. As Martin Gallent, zoning attorney and former Chairman of the Planning Commission, told us: "The problem is, I guess, that the City could not make up its mind whether it was the chief builder of the city or the chief planner of the city."

It is rumored that there might be an interesting relationship between the Coliseum site and the Special Midtown District, which was adopted in May, 1982. As we shall discuss in detail in Chapter 6, the principal goal of the Midtown district was to decrease building size on the East Side of mid-Manhattan by lowering the FAR in that area and to encourage development west of Fifth Avenue by increasing the FAR from 15 to 18 on that side of the district for five years. If you examine the map of the Midtown district on page 78, you will see that the district is roughly shaped like a rectangle running south from Central Park South to 31st Street and east from Eighth Avenue to Third Avenue. One deviation from this shape is the curious bulb at the corner at 59th Street and Seventh Avenue that extends to embrace the Coliseum site. Is it possible that in May, 1982, when the Midtown district was adopted, the City already knew that it would be disposing of the site? Might the City have noted that the benefits to any land included on the West Side of the district would be greater allowed density...and a greater price for the land? The former City planners we asked about this say that the overlap of the Midtown district was purely motivated by planning concerns. According to John Zuccotti,

> The decision to include the Coliseum site in the Special Midtown District was made as part of the comprehensive planning and environmental studies undertaken in connection with the creation of the district. One of the principal goals of the District was to encourage development in the western area of Midtown, and the Coliseum site was viewed as the northern anchor for Eighth Avenue....The Coliseum site was rezoned with the understanding that it would be redeveloped. There is no reason to think that the decision to rezone was motivated by financial considerations rather than legitimate planning criteria.[10]

If financial consideration had influenced the rezoning, it might have been an abuse of the purpose of a special district.

The Coliseum fiasco was the result of simple greed and clever boundary drawing. There were few conditions, guidelines, or standards set out in the Request for Proposal—besides brief mentions of economic viability and non-specific "benefits" to the City—the main request was clearly just the highest price, please. It illustrates the Koch administration's approach to economic development and urban planning, an approach that had a major effect on the creation and administration of special districts. This story also indicates a source of the City–citizen conflicts that play a large part in the history of some New York special districts. Kent Barwick tells us that there would have been no lawsuit if the City had set bulk and height conditions and received a bid of, say, $300 million.

1990 and Beyond: the New City Government

As we mentioned at the start of this chapter, today the structure of the government of New York City is dramatically different. There is a new Mayor, David Dinkins, who took office January 1, 1990, the same day the changes came into effect. It is too early to tell what type of policies will be established under Mayor Dinkins. A speech before a campaign breakfast sponsored by the Municipal Art Society on July 12, 1989, may give us a clue. Mr. Dinkins said:

> You have sought to preserve a reasonable, human-scale environment, consistent with the City's economically integrated traditions. I share your commitment and I deplore the policies of the City Planning Commission, which have encouraged too many undistinguished megadevelopments, seemingly based on no value other than the dollars to be generated by maximum floor area.
>
> Manhattan real estate has become such a hot market that the sheer magnitude of the money involved appears to overwhelm any balanced value system. And we know that overdevelopment brings with it real costs: the loss of air and light, wear and tear on urban infrastructure, pedestrian and vehicle gridlock, and the inability of sanitation and transportation services to keep up with new demands.[11]

Mayor Dinkins is working within a different City government than did his predecessors due to the restructuring that was ordered in 1989. The catalyst for these changes was a dispute over the role of the Board of Estimate. On March 22, 1989, the United States Supreme court held unanimously in *Board of Estimate of City of New York v. Morris* that the Board was invalid because it violated the one-person–one-vote doctrine.[12] For example, Brooklyn has a population of 2,230,936 and Staten Island has 352,151, yet each had one member on the Board of Estimate. We can't help but wonder why it took so long for someone to bring such a case; twenty-five years had gone by since the first one-person–one-vote decision (*Reynolds v. Sims*, 377 U.S. 533 (1965)).

The *Morris* decision forced the City to appoint a Commission to redraft the charter. The new charter was submitted to the voters and approved in November, 1989, at the same time the electorate chose David Dinkins as their new Mayor. The Commission proposed, and the voters endorsed, the abolition of the Board of Estimate. All legislative power was vested instead in the City Council, which consists of thirty-five members. This number will be expanded to fifty-one members in a special election in 1991 after the 1990 census.

One can imagine the lobbying that went on before the Charter Revision Commission. Regarding the redistribution of planning and permitting power, one report noted:

> Urban planning advocates wanted to seize the charter revision opportunity to structure comprehensive planning into city government. It seemed possible in the new charter to integrate an independent planning agency that set a long-term agenda for issues like infrastructure, housing, education, and health care with revitalized and empowered community planning boards that implemented this agenda at a local level.[13]

The same report summed up the Commission's goal:

> However, a priority for the Charter Commission was somehow to recreate the Board of Estimate's distribution of power among citywide and borough officials, and the City Planning Commission was the locus for accomplishing this. Thus, the proposed Planning Commission con-

sists of seven appointees by the Mayor and one ap-
pointee each by the five borough presidents and the City
Council president. The appointees can be removed only
by the respective appointing official, and one can reasonably project that the commissioners will represent that
official's point of view.[14]

This arrangement appears to make the Planning Commission even more political than it has been. Instead of a group
of appointees who could at least be expected to reflect the
agenda of the mayor who appointed them, city planning will
be overseen by a group of people with widely divergent agendas and priorities—possibly standing in the way of good comprehensive planning.

A possible counter to this potential is an interesting provision in the new charter meant to cure the NIMBY paralysis
in site selection for City facilities. The charter calls for the
Planning Commission to draft rules for the "fair distribution"
of benefits and burdens among the communities. The Mayor
then will annually issue a citywide statement of needs. In
each statement, the Mayor will ask the Planning Commission
to approve sites for such pariahs as homeless shelters or in-
cinerators. Each site must be consistent with the "fair distribution" rules. The Borough President may propose an alternative site, but it must also comply with these rules. The
above report says: "Although a community might always resist a facility it does not like, it should no longer have the argument that the location is irrational and unfair."[15]

This provision is probably the most exciting of all the
changes in the Charter. If it works, it may be the most efficient way to resolve the age-old conflict between City Hall
and the neighborhoods over the location of public facilities,
many of which are not considered good neighbors.

Conclusion

New York City has passed through hell and back between the administrations of Lindsay and Koch. After near
bankruptcy, the City underwent a boom and a budget sur-

plus but is now once again in dismal financial straits. The results of this seesawing fortune are the inheritance of a low-
key Mayor, David Dinkins, who must be to New Yorkers, at
least for the time, rather relaxing after Edward Koch.

Special zoning districts are part of the Lindsay–Koch
heritage, and their history reflects the very different attitudes
of these two Mayors. Probably the most remarkable feature of
the zoning regulatory system in New York City is that special
districts not only survived but spread during two such different administrations. The creative planning idea advocated by
Lindsay endured the assault of Koch's total indifference to
planning and, as we shall see, was even used to further
Koch's pro-development ends. Viewed from the brightest
perch, the survival of special districts suggests that they have
strength; more likely, it just reflects Koch's neglect.

Perhaps the most significant fact about this era of contrast is that people have become more sensitive to zoning
practice regardless of the Mayor's attitude. Many Community Boards are active and numerous groups now rally
around a special district any time there is an effort to change
the rules.

The Theater District

An Idea Is Born

The whole subject of zoning was a revelation to us. It had always seemed a very dreary subject, of little relevance to any creative endeavor. As a result of our experience with the theater district, we came to realize that zoning could be made into one of the basic methods of designing cities.

Jonathan Barnett
Urban Design as Public Policy, 1974

Most visitors to New York came for one or more of three purposes: to either "do a deal" with lawyers and bankers; scan the garment market for the latest designs; or just be entertained—usually meaning the legitimate theater. They still come to make deals (although fewer since the Wall Street scandals), but the garment industry has fallen on hard times, even though the International Ladies Garment Workers Union still enjoys significant political clout. The theater industry, too, has been in a continual state of decline since the 1930s, occasionally interrupted by a success imported from England. Still, in spite of its downhill slide, the Broadway theater area remains the largest and most famous concentration of legitimate theaters in the world. The special district phenomenon in New York first arose from the City's attempts to save this fading star.

Background

The origins of the present theater district go back to the turn of this century, when the theater business moved north into the area now known as Times Square. In the first decade of this century, "the method of presenting a play was undergoing a fundamental change. The 'stock system,' whereby actors worked in one theater for a season in a variety of plays, was replaced by the 'combination system,' under which a company of actors appearing in a single show would tour from city to city. Important to the viability of the combination system was a single location to cast, rehearse, and develop a show for a cross-country tour. New York became the headquarters for the combination system."[1] Most of today's theaters were built during this time (between 1901 and 1927), stretching along 42nd Street and up Broadway past Times Square.

This boom ended with the Depression. By the 1930s, the number of theaters in the Times Square area had dropped to sixty-eight from almost 100 at the beginning of the century. Many were torn down or converted to movie houses, leaving about thirty by 1950. Since then, more theaters have given way to hotels or office buildings. When an old theater was destroyed, it was rarely replaced with a new one. From 1930 to 1960, there were no new legitimate theaters constructed. Gerald Schoenfeld, Chairman of Shubert Theaters, Inc., which owns about seventeen theaters, told us some of the reasons for this:

> Nobody will build a theater. I was just saying, assuming that you could, you would never be able to build a theater like these. That's what I'm saying. Nobody will build a theater. And these theaters are dying buildings. Economically obsolete in many instances. All between sixty and eighty years of age. And yet intended to be maintained and preserved through some economic miracle.

The danger to the theaters was that they were extremely uneconomic uses of land. Those that survived into the second half of the twentieth century did so only because they were totally depreciated and paid relatively low taxes.

The theaters were three-story buildings with an FAR of approximately 4 sitting in the middle of an area that had a zoned FAR of 15 that, with extravagant bonuses, could be manipulated to over 21 FAR. "Old Broadway" could not compete with all that unused FAR in a developer's heart. As the towers went up, the theater district was disappearing.

The Paradox of Times Square

We should drop a little more hot pepper into this stew: the troublesome position of Times Square, located within the theater district at the intersection of Seventh Avenue and Broadway just north of 42nd Street. Since World War II, 42nd Street between Seventh and Eighth Avenues had become a hellhole of prostitutes, drug pushers, porno shops, and cut-rate stores of every variety. And Times Square had become just as tawdry. According to Brendan Gill of the *New Yorker*, "G.K. Chesterton said once of the gaudy bedazzlement of Times Square at night that it would be a paradise for anyone lucky enough to be unable to read."[2] But to many thousands around the nation, the place was still considered synonymous with Manhattan; like a magnet, it drew tourists to its glitz and its sleaze.

Each in its own fashion, both West 42nd Street and Times Square were an embarrassment to City Hall. Mayor after mayor growled over this area like a dog with an old bone. For at least twenty-five years, the planning staff and, later, the New York State Urban Development Corporation tinkered with plans to clean up both areas and put them more in keeping with the sterile Sixth Avenue (Avenue of the Americas) and posh Fifth Avenue to the east. Every plan for redeveloping the area was met with cries of protest from guardians of the public weal—the *New York Times*, the Metropolitan Art Society, and just plain nostalgists such as Brendan Gill of the *New Yorker*. In 1987, Gill wrote:

> Given its location at the center of overcrowded, overbuilt-upon Manhattan, Times Square at present is a remarkably open and airy space, from which much sky is

visible; sunlight readily penetrates the skeletal frames of
the great illuminated signs for which it is celebrated—
signs that perch on buildings modest in height and
agreeably ramshackle in appearance.[3]

The comfortable scale and honky-tonk fame of Times
Square was an important part of the theater district's ambience. But the sleaze and decay also gave the district a bad
name. The question became how to clean up the area without
driving out the theaters.

Catalyst: One Astor Plaza

When John Lindsay's crew of urban designers arrived
on the scene in 1967, one of the first crises they encountered
was a proposal by Sam Minskoff & Sons, a large developer, to
tear down the old Astor Hotel on the west side of Times
Square and erect a high-rise office building. Minskoff
thought that he had already obtained the Planning Commission's agreement to grant him a special permit that would allow him to build a tower without setbacks, something he
could not have done as-of-right.

Jonathan Barnett, one of Lindsay's designers-planners-
architects, recounted the initial reaction of the Urban Design
Group to this situation in his book *Urban Design as Public
Policy*: "I wish I could say that we all immediately under-
stood that the real question wasn't the building on the site of
the Astor Hotel but the future of New York's theatrical district. That was the basic issue, all right, but it took us some
time before we realized it."[4] Barnett explained:

> People on the outside tend to assume that planning com-
> missions understand exactly what they are doing when
> they make a zoning change, just as we expect that the
> Federal Reserve Bank, or the President's Council of Eco-
> nomic Advisors, fully understand the consequences of
> their actions. In fact, however, the issues involved are so
> complicated that it is hard to predict the chain of events
> that these kinds of decisions set off. When the Planning
> Commission first considered the zoning adjustments

that would enable the Minskoff firm to build on the west side of Broadway, it thought more of the consequences to the city as a whole than of the effect of the building on the complex of land uses immediately around it.

Our first reaction to the building as urban designers was much more in terms of its immediate surroundings. We were concerned about the future of Times Square, which, despite its tawdry aspects, has great symbolic value as the center of night life in the big city, as is shown by the number of tourists who make a point of going there when they visit New York.[5]

Two things were clear: the Times Square area was losing theaters, and Minskoff wanted a big building. Could the City solve both problems by having Minskoff put a legitimate theater in the new building? The planners and the developer embarked on an interminable series of meetings and conferences. The planning staff's suggestion that the builder add a legitimate theater to the project was greeted, Barnett told us, "with derision." The developer tried going over the staff's head by requesting a meeting with the Mayor. Fine, said the Mayor, call Donald Elliott, Chairman of the Planning Commission, to arrange such a meeting.[6] To politically savvy developers, this was a new twist: political power in the Lindsay administration was not going to ignore the planners. According to Barnett, the developer retreated a bit and protested that a theater in a high rise was not impractical, just expensive. Actually, no one knew what a theater on the third floor of a high rise would cost. Naturally, the City thus did not know what kind of bonus FAR to offer the developer as an incentive to go through with this scheme.

Birth of a Special District

It was Norman Marcus, the long-time General Counsel to the Planning Commission, who came up with the idea of putting in a special zoning district between Sixth and Eighth Avenues and from 40th Street to 57th Street. Norman is a brilliant, imaginative lawyer, but we doubt that even he knew

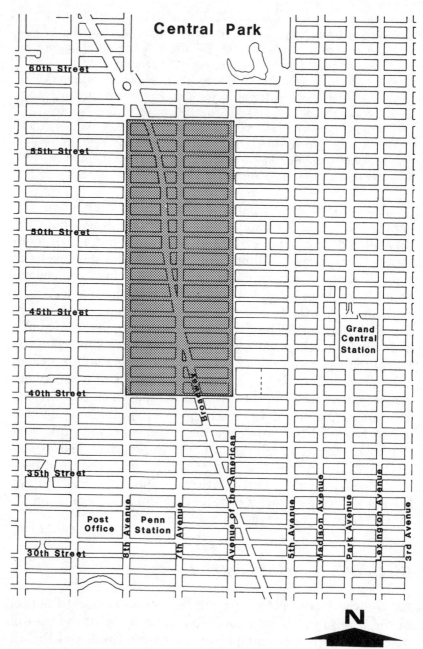

1967 Special Theater District, New York City.
Source: *New York City Planning Commission*

what he had spawned. The idea seemed to be simple: get developers in that district to include new theaters in their projects by giving them a bonus FAR. This, to him, appeared to solve a number of legal and practical problems. The district was large enough to avoid the charge of spot zoning; it did not mandate the building of theaters; and it did not offer the same bonus anywhere else in Manhattan. According to Marcus, this last was an important consideration: "We didn't want to create a sorcerer's apprentice where everybody would be building theaters, which would have been stupid."

The rub was that no one knew how much bonus FAR to give in return for one theater. The planners didn't know what to offer the developer; the developer didn't know what the open span of a theater would cost. They finally settled on a bonus of an additional 20 percent FAR. In a conversation in 1987, Donald Elliott, former Chairman of the Planning Commission, offered an explanation for how the bonus amount was reached:

DE   We wanted it to essentially maintain the preexisting value of the land, slightly more but not an enormous windfall. On the other hand, we didn't want it to be a punishment because it was voluntary; we could not require it. It was an incentive that somebody had to be willing to build. We put a lot of pressure on the Minskoffs, so while it was voluntary, we were fairly tough about trying to get it to occur. Our best judgment was that we made a mistake of about $1 million on that building.

RFB Over, gave them more?

DE   We gave them about a million more in value. It was offset, interestingly enough, because they were convinced that the theater cost them about $1 million more than expected. So they were equally unknowledgeable.

Norman Marcus himself gave us the explanation that probably best reflects the arbitrary nature of the final number: "Why 20 percent? The answer lies in anthropology."

Even with the new district bonus in place, One Astor Plaza got a theater only after interminable negotiations. The

City was probably able to get Minskoff to sit down at the bargaining table only because the project needed a special permit from the City. Once the developer finally agreed to the theater, the Planning Commission requested, and received, a grant from the Ford Foundation to hire a committee of theater experts to set guidelines for its construction.

1967 Special Theater District in Action

The idea may be said to have worked. As the high-rise office buildings moved in, the City got four new theaters in addition to the Minskoff: the Marquis Theater in the Mariott–Marquis Hotel; the Gershwin and Circle in the Square in the Uris Building; and the American Place in the Stevens Building.

One can hardly get the same kick from taking an elevator to the third floor of an office building or hotel to go to see a play as one does from entering a ground floor of an old theater, and it is true that some of the new theaters have a barnlike atmosphere. But certainly the lobbies are more spacious; you don't have to rub a stranger's fanny as you gasp for air or go out into the street to light a cigarette. And, undoubtedly, the backstage facilities are less medieval.

Yet, there was a basic incongruity in all this: office towers presented the greatest threat to the ambience and vitality of the Times Square area, but the only way to get a new theater was to help a developer build an office tower. Perhaps giving new high rises a bonus FAR was not the way to save the theater district. A growing public sensitivity to urban design issues and the emergence of the preservation movement led to change in the special district regulations.

1982 Revision

Succumbing to citizen pressure to curb the growth of towers in mid-Manhattan, the City created the Special Midtown District on May 13, 1982 (see Chapter 6 for a full discussion).

The new Marquis Theater in the Marriott Hotel, Special Theater District.
Photo: *John Babcock*

It embraced both the Special Theater District and the Special Fifth Avenue District, which became Special Subdistricts.

The Midtown rezoning made major changes in the regulations of the theater district, prompted no doubt by the demolition in March, 1982, of the Helen Hayes and Belasco Theaters to make room for a hotel. Public demonstrations were ignited by fears that other theaters would disappear.

In the new Theater Subdistrict, the 1967 bonus for putting a theater in an office building was removed. The most striking change in the regulations was the listing of forty-four theaters as landmarks, which could only be demolished by obtaining a City Planning Commission special permit after meeting specified criteria. In order to grant the special permit, the Commission had to find that:

1. Demolition of the theaters will not harm the entertainment section of the City's economy;
2. The theater needs substantial rehabilitation but is not eligible for tax abatement or other public assistance;
3. The theater is not capable of providing a reasonable return; and
4. There is a plan for new development on the zoning lot which...will include a new theater or theater supportive uses.[7]

The listed theaters (see Appendix B) were somewhat compensated for landmark designation by being given the right to transfer development rights (TDRs) to adjacent lots, either contiguous, across a street and opposite, or catercorner to the landmark lot. In addition, a Theater Retention Bonus was created. Under this provision, a theater owner may sell the theater's zoned rights to build extra floor area to the developer of a non-contiguous site located within the subdistrict, provided that the theater owner covenants to maintain and retain the theater for legitimate theater use. This bonus works independently of the transfer of landmark TDRs. A designated theater may sell its landmark TDRs to an adjacent site *and* sell its Retention Bonus to a noncontiguous site in the theater subdistrict. Apparently, many of the landmark theaters have taken advantage of these provisions.

In many ways, these new provisions were tougher and more restrictive than the earlier regulations. In part, this was because of the influence of the Landmarks Commission, created in 1965. The landmarking of forty-four theaters made it much less likely that they would be replaced by high rises. But even these tougher provisions did not solve everything. The new district could not prevent new high rises on other parcels, but it could ensure that the existing theaters remain intact despite changes in their surroundings.

Legal Challenge

In spite of all the applause the City received for its action, one group was unhappy: the theater owners. On June 20, 1988, eleven organizations, including Shubert Theaters, Inc. and the Nederlander organization, filed suit. They alleged that the landmarking of forty-four theaters was *ultra vires*, the designation of an entire industry, not of specific buildings; that the designation of landmark interiors in some theaters was capricious and could interfere with necessary production changes; that the designation was subject to environmental review; and that the designation was an unconstitutional taking. There were other counts in their complaint as well. They concluded by asking for $200 million in damages.

Briefs were filed, and after a hearing, the trial judge dismissed all counts of the complaint after the City's motion for summary judgment. The plaintiffs have filed an appeal.

Times Square Redevelopment

The 1982 Midtown revisions may be seen as a compromise between the public's desire to save the theater district and the Koch administration's intent to milk the last dime of taxable values out of the city's real estate. Rather than ease the economic pressure on the theaters by lowering the zoned FAR for the entire district, the City used landmarking and TDRs to allow development to go on as usual except on the parcels occupied by the forty-four landmarked theaters. Critics might argue that surrounding the theaters with towers will be just as detrimental to their survival as knocking them down; the special ambience and attraction of the theater district will be lost forever.

Nothing better illustrates this conflict over the theater district between the City and the citizens than the redevelopment of Times Square at the south end of the Special Theater District. We have mentioned City Hall's embarrassment over the condition of Times Square and West 42nd Street. Plans for redoing these areas were redrawn and revised until, in the mid-1980s, it appeared that a workable scheme had evolved. The plan was to erect four high-rise office buildings on Times Square and to completely eliminate the junk on West 42nd Street by condemnation, tax breaks to developers, and milking the zoning ordinance for every possible bonus. Gill described this scheme in the *New Yorker*:

> Thanks to a formula that, as far as I know, had never been used before, which allowed all areas within the boundaries of the thirteen-acre project to be dealt with as a single building site, the Burgee–Johnson towers were granted densities greater than any other New York City buildings had ever been permitted to possess. The current maximum FAR for the Times Square area is eighteen and is reckoned to be too high; it is soon to be reduced, perhaps to fifteen. The Burgee–Johnson tower planned for the northeast corner of Forty-second Street and Broadway would occupy a site of thirty-three thousand square feet and would contain a million and a half square feet of space—an FAR of forty-five![8]

Forty-second Street was also to be transformed into a line of office towers with some type of a merchandise mart at the northeast corner of the street and Eighth Avenue.

This plan is now being implemented. The City and the New York State Urban Development Corporation have thrown a couple of sops to the advocates of the old, garish Times Square. The tower at One Times Square Plaza, the funny triangular structure that carries the latest headlines in lighted movable letters around its sides like a series of giant, illuminated billboards will apparently remain, though dwarfed by the thirty-one and fifty-eight story buildings that will surround it. The other bone that has been tossed to the old order is a requirement that the new buildings provide bracelets of illuminated signs around their skins, a proposal not greeted with enthusiasm by the developers who feared that two or three floors encased in neon would result in lower rentals.

Ada Louise Huxtable, former architecture critic for the *New York Times*, uttered the malediction on this development in 1987: "The Times Square Redevelopment Plan is part of the [City's] same spread-sheet syndrome, but it lacks the beautiful simplicity of the direct sell-off and relies more on circuitous giveaways. A joint city–state exercise, it calls for the kind of bulldozer renewal that was universally repudiated after the 1960s. This destructive, wrongheaded, highly profitable project hooked up to a 42nd Street cleanup, which no one denies is needed."[9]

Huxtable went on to criticize the City's approach in more detail:

> To achieve this end, there will be enormous office towers created through zoning calisthenics that merge several building lots in a single calculation, the dislocation of neighborhoods, people and skills, and a sanitizing operation that will gentrify and homogenize Times Square and help the theater district on its way to extinction. Design guidelines provided by the city were summarily discarded by the developer, and his architects who correctly sensed that no one in charge would challenge the default. The towers themselves, oversized commercial packages wrapped in a bit of quasi-historical trim by Johnson and Burgee, are a curious blend of the gross and the effete.
>
> The Times Square scheme goes beyond simple greed to more serious delinquencies—from willfully wrong assumptions about what creates and nurtures a city's life to failure to acknowledge changes that make a plan invalid or undesirable.[10]

There was much more criticism of the Times Square redevelopment. So the architect, John Burgee, went back to the

drawing board and in August, 1989, submitted yet another proposal. The four office towers would be just as dense and tall,
ranging from thirty-two to fifty-seven stories and making up
4.1 million square feet. Because of the many public demands
that the structures reflect the neon and honky-tonk of Times
Square, the new buildings incorporate setbacks, cutbacks, an-
gled roofs, reflected surfaces in blue and green glass, and built-
in multicolored neon signs. Paul Goldberger in the *Times* of
September 1, 1989, wrote: "They are as different from the now
cookie-cutter classicism of the previous project as Disneyland is
from the Albany Mall."[11] But Goldberger also pointed out:

> The bad news is that this is all cosmetics. For the problem
> with the original design was never just the way it looked,
> bad as that was; it was the fact that the towers were too
> big and too bulky, and threatened to put what little is left
> of Times Square and the theater district into shadow....
> These new buildings are just as big, and just as bulky.[12]

The City will have its towers and its cleaned-up Times
Square. Its effect on the theater district remains to be seen.

Conclusion

The Special Theater District was the first attempt in
New York City to expand zoning to protect a specific kind of
use. The original 1967 district was not entirely successful because it used the wrong tools: instead of preserving the old
theaters, the incentives encouraged their destruction. The
verdict is still out on the 1982 Midtown revision. Yet, despite
the fact that in this first experiment the means did not quite
produce the desired ends, the special district idea caught on.

The Special Theater District's greatest impact was on
the city as a whole. Jonathan Barnett, in *An Introduction to
Urban Design*, likened the fate of special zoning districts to
that of penicillin: "When penicillin was first introduced, it acquired a reputation as a 'miracle drug' and was prescribed in
many situations for which it was not appropriate."[13] The special district was a new device that could be applied elsewhere; in the years to come, it was, with passion but not always careful consideration of the consequences.

Clinton

Preserving Hell's Kitchen

Clinton's basic problem is not its housing, which is old, nor its population, which is declining, nor its average income, which is low. The essential problem is its location. Were it located almost anywhere else in the City, it would be a model for low-income communities. As it happens, Clinton is sitting on what may become, in the relatively near future, some of the most valuable land in New York City.

Weiner/Gran Associates
Clinton: A Plan for Preservation, 1974

Clinton 3, Mayors 0

"Let me tell you something about Clinton. There are more dead mayors' bodies littered around that place that have tried to tangle with Clinton than any single area of the city. [Clinton's people] beat Lindsay. They beat Beame and they knocked Koch out. They never lost."

Considering the economic and social conditions in the area of mid-Manhattan now known as Clinton and its depressed, almost sordid history, this is a remarkable statement. Clinton is a low-income neighborhood that occupies the west side of mid-Manhattan from West 43rd Street to West 56th Street and from the west side of Eighth Avenue to the Hudson River. It lies chock-a-block the towers of Midtown yet consists mainly of Old Law tenements—four- or five-story, pre-1901 buildings that offer a living experience akin to residing in an elevator shaft and having a garbage

chute for light and air. We asked Martin Gallent, attorney
and former ten-year Vice-Chairman of the New York City
Planning Commission (as well as the commentator quoted in
the first paragraph of this chapter), how this apparently depressed area, Clinton, had defeated the plans of three succes-
sive New York mayors. Here was his explanation.

RFB Why did you say [Clinton's people] beat Lindsay?
MG   Lindsay wanted to recreate that whole area. Look
     in the Master Plan of 1969. In the Master Plan of
     1969, he denigrated that area, said this is a terri-
     ble area; this is Hell's Kitchen. This is awful. We're
     going to redo this. Then they knocked out his plan.
RFB Beame likewise?
MG   Beame also tried to knock out parts of Hell's
     Kitchen. They wouldn't have it happen.
RFB And where did they get Koch?
MG   The most recent one. This was 1986. City Plan-
     ning approved an urban renewal development
     there. The community [people] came in with their
     own plan. They went to the Board of Estimate and
     got the votes. And Koch withdrew. At first he
     wouldn't listen to their plan. Then he said the
     plan was no good through his agents. They
     stonewalled them and then when they got to the
     Board of Estimate, he got clobbered.
RFB Clinton isn't what remains of the old political
     power here, is it?
MG   No. The marvelous thing is there are always new
     people. In each one of these instances under the
     Mayor, there were new people who came up and
     said no. It is the most incredible thing about this
     area that there is a regeneration of community in-
     terest and concern and leadership. Now the leader-
     ship that knocked Koch out is not the same leader-
     ship that knocked Lindsay out. There is something
     in the water there that breeds very tough people.

The history of the Special Clinton District is a David-and-
Goliath story of how neighborhood residents preserved affordable housing for another generation by forcing the City
to do something to mitigate pressures caused by its own de-

velopment activities. Clinton is unique among the special districts we studied in its use of zoning to achieve explicit affordable housing goals.

Background

Today, Clinton is inhabited by an ethnic mix of Germans, Irish, and Puerto Ricans. Many tenants are descendants of immigrants who settled in the neighborhood at the beginning of this century. First settled by Irish and Germans after the Civil War, Clinton until around 1940 was known as Hell's Kitchen and was scourged by gangs: the Tenth Avenue Gang, the Hudson Dusters, the Dead Rabbits, and—most notorious—the Hell's Kitchen Gang.

Clinton is still poor. Excluding one census tract (139), the average family income was $8,900 in 1974[1] and probably has not risen much since then. People live and work in a small area, just as they did a century ago. In 1970, approximately 34 percent of the residents walked to work, twice the average for New York City. Clinton is cheek-by-jowl with the theater district and Times Square, and many of its residents work at low-paying jobs in the theater trade—ushers, stage hands, and concessionaires.

The primary form of housing in the neighborhood is the "Old Law" tenement building. The 1974 report, *Clinton: A Plan for Preservation*, described the origins of these tenements.

Throughout the nineteenth century, prominent New York citizens were periodically seized with a need to instigate tenement reform. In 1866, the first law was enacted to regulate tenement houses. It required stairways to have banisters, multiple dwellings to have fire escapes, and a water closet or outside privy for every twenty tenants. The Board of Health ordered transoms cut in 46,000 unventilated rooms in 1869. A second law, passed in 1879, limited the percentage of a lot which could be occupied by buildings and stated that no room could be used for sleeping unless it had a window opening onto a street or court. A prize competition for model

tenements resulted in the design of the "dumbbell" tenement or "railroad flat" with narrow airshafts. Many
buildings of this type remain standing in Clinton today.[2]

Development Pressures

The pressure first came on this unlikely area, this
throwback to the nineteenth Century, in the midst of the
mid-Manhattan high-rise boom of the early 1970s. The
neighborhood lost many of its Old Law tenement buildings,
not because the residents wanted to move, but because of development pressure from the East Side of Manhattan. Ab-
sentee landlords of rent-controlled old buildings used every
means of harassment to force tenants out, including putting
prostitutes and addicts into abandoned apartments.

This development pressure continues today. On March
2, 1987, the *New York Daily News* reported:

> Bodegas that once lined Ninth Ave. are quickly disap-
> pearing due to massive rent increases, only to be replaced
> by trendy restaurants, unisex hair salons, and boutiques.
> Young professionals are moving into renovated tenement
> apartments that rent for more than $1,200 a month,
> while many long-time merchants worry that they will
> have to close up shop when their leases expire.[3]

The flag of fear first went up when the Lindsay administration announced in 1972 that a convention center would be
built on the Hudson River at 47th Street. Now, Clinton
would be squeezed from the west as well as the east. Cries of
outrage were heard all the way down to City Hall. Clinton
would be in danger of more traffic, pollution, and—worst of
all—gentrification, as had already begun to occur in Census
Tract 139 in the northeast corner of the neighborhood.

Clinton's Political Resources

Clinton was not without resources to fight this fate.
These resources were political. Besides the constantly re-

Clinton, looking east on West 44th Street.
Photo: *John Babcock*

newed resident activism Gallent mentioned above, Clinton also had a powerful survivor of the old-style political system. Jean Lerman, who had worked in Clinton as Director of the Neighborhood Preservation Office, described how traditional political power worked in Clinton:

> The political leader, who is still the political leader, Jimmy McManus, heads a club named for his grand un-cle or something, Eugene McManus, who started the club as a reformer in about 1901 kicking out Plun-ketts....McManus was the one who took over, and the Irish, with the longshoremen, really were the mainstay of Clinton, and they stayed there in those tenements all those years, and Jimmy always was able to deliver his X number of votes to whomever....He was part of an old-line kind of Democratic organization who had a strong service-orientation to the community—taking care of in-

dividual people's problems and favors and finding people
jobs. He was really an old time kind of district leader. In
the 1960s, sweeping the entire West and East Sides of
Manhattan and Greenwich Village was the reform
Democratic movement that came out of Stevenson and
then Kennedy that defeated just about every old-line
regular...organization except Jimmy McManus. Couldn't
budge that constituency because the ones who voted
there lived in Old Law tenements. It's climbing a lot of
stairs. In fact, Jimmy's people fought a lot of new housing in the community for years because they really didn't
want a new group of people coming in who they didn't
control. They stayed in power. They are in power until
this very day. Jimmy McManus is still in power.

There were other political forces at work for Clinton.
Part of the planned convention center would be built out into
the Hudson River. In order to get a permit to do this, the City
had to obtain a finding from Congress that the river was non-
navigable. The Hudson River non-navigable! As it happened,
Clinton's Congresswoman Bella Abzug was on the key committee. In her usual subtle manner, she informed the New
York City Planning Commission that there was no way such a
finding would be forthcoming unless something was done to
protect the character of Clinton. Added to her insistence were
the demands of Community Board No. 4 for some assurance
that Clinton would be protected from the threatened on-
slaught from the west. Clearly, something had to be done.

Months of meetings and negotiations between the community and City Hall began. John Zuccotti, then Chairman
of the Planning Commission, was, according to all accounts,
a brilliant bargainer. He came to be beloved by the folks in
Clinton. According to Norman Marcus, former General Counsel to the Planning Commission:

> They loved him. I'll never forget one night at one of these
> meetings at around midnight. There are many priests in
> this community. There are a lot of Roman Catholic
> churches. There is an Irish background there. I mention
> that because Zuccotti ran out of cigarettes one night and
> one of the women who was at the meeting, a middle-aged
> woman, looked at him and said, "If it's okay, Father
> Zuccotti, I'll run down and get cigarettes for you."

Zuccotti's special talent was to accommodate himself to the neighborhood's unique needs and style. The negotiation process in Clinton in some ways resembled the clash of two different cultures. Norman Marcus described the climate of these meetings:

> Clinton was a political district. It also happened to be a fascinating community that was not at all well-known to planners....Planners were all very middle class and didn't come from areas like Clinton. For example, you couldn't meet with this community except at eleven o'clock at night when everybody got off their hotel shift or wherever they were working. The planners had gotten up at nine o'clock in the morning and gone to the office, and then they had to go to this eleven o'clock meeting, which didn't end until about one or two. It just was simply not the same rhythm, but for that reason it was very interesting.

In Clinton, the Planning Commission was facing a neighborhood on the cusp of a political revolt. So, in addition to the innumerable meetings chaired by John Zuccotti, the Commission hired the planning firm of Weiner/Gran Associates to undertake a major analysis of the economics, housing, and demographics of Clinton. Their 1974 report supported the idea of creating one more special district.

The Special Clinton District

The Planning Commission had recommended early in the process that an interim special district be put in place for one year to counteract a possible rush to the Building Department by developers while a final plan for Clinton was hammered out. The Special Interim Preservation District, which was adopted by the Board of Estimate in 1973, imposed a temporary moratorium on development in Clinton. The 1973 report that recommended the Special Interim Preservation District described the process:

> This special district legislation represents a new experiment in the working relationships between city government and a local community. It is a relationship in

which municipal government has given full recognition
to the burdens that can be placed on a community in
which a large-scale, citywide facility is to be located. The
approach focuses on the need to respond to the special
requirements of such a neighborhood....The Special Interim Preservation District for Clinton was created over
a long period by joint efforts of the Planning Commission
and an active community steering committee, which includes members of Community Board No. 4 and the
Clinton Planning Council. The district helps protect the
mixed-income residential community and local shops
from pressures generated by the Convention Center on
the west and an expanding central business district on
the east. It is one of several actions being taken to
strengthen the area in the face of rising land values,
land assemblages, and speculation.[4]

The permanent Special Clinton District was approved
by the Planning Commission a year later on October 21,
1974, and was passed by the Board of Estimate on November
1, 1974. The community had won.

The Special Clinton District is unusual because it is the
only example we know of a district primarily created to protect affordable housing. The major provisions of the district
work towards this end in a variety of ways. The "General Purposes" of the district explicitly state that special programs are
needed to handle the effects of development pressures from
the east and west. The goals for the Clinton area include:

1. To preserve and strengthen the residential character
   of the community;
2. To permit rehabilitation and new construction within
   the area in character with the existing scale of the
   community and at rental levels *which will not substantially alter the mixture of income groups presently
   residing in the area*; (emphasis added)
3. To preserve the small-scale character and variety of
   existing stores and activities and to control new commercial uses in conformity with the existing character of the area;
4. To provide amenities such as public open space and
   street trees to improve the physical environment;

5. To restrict demolition of buildings that are suitable for rehabilitation and continued residential use; and

6. To promote the most desirable use of land in the area and thus to conserve the value of land and buildings, and thereby protect the City's tax revenues, consistent with the foregoing purposes.[5]

The district is divided into four subareas. The Preservation Area, by far the largest, occupies the core twenty-five blocks of the district. In this area, the floor area ratio for residential buildings is limited to 4.2, meaning that buildings can only be five or six stories tall. Demolition of sound buildings is prohibited without a special permit from both the Planning Commission and the Board of Estimate. In order to get the permit, the owner has to prove there had been no harassment to induce tenants to leave, a provision that has caused legal difficulties. New and rehabilitated buildings had to have three and a half rooms per unit on the average, with at least 20 percent of these units being four-and-a-half-room apartments.

On the south side of the district, there is a Perimeter Area, which permits higher density residential use. If developers rehabilitate buildings in the Preservation Area and maintain rent control in them at $37 per room, they receive a floor area bonus they may use for a project in the Perimeter Area. The Mixed Use Area, a small section along Tenth Avenue, allows the continuance of mixed industrial and residential use already there. In the "Other Areas" subdistrict, the original underlying zoning remains.

The district also has additional provisions for mandatory tree plantings. Exquisitely detailed provisions for public parking lots were incorporated into the ordinance, including a provision that existing public parking lots had the right to continue only for five years and thereafter would be terminated unless a special permit was granted.

Only one major developer in the area outfoxed Clinton when the district boundaries were being drawn: William Zeckendorf. He had his eye on a parcel on the east side of the proposed district that had been the site of the old Madison Square Garden before it was torn down. Zeckendorf & Com-

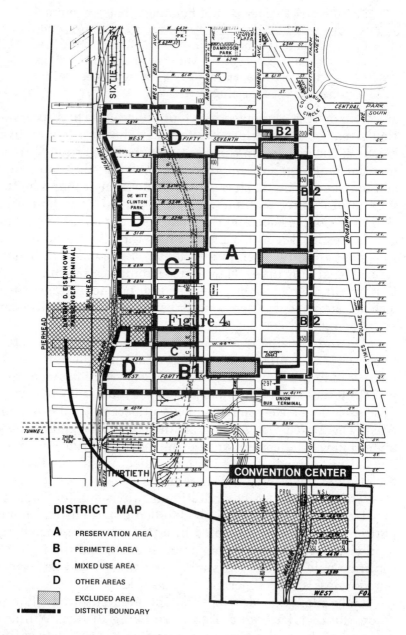

Special Clinton District.
Source: *New York City Planning Commission*

pany bought the site from Gulf & Western and then acquired six other sites that were occupied by old, vacant buildings. Zeckendorf offered to refurbish these other buildings as low-rent apartments if, in return, Clinton would agree to exclude the Madison Square Garden site from the special district. The Clinton people, after much bargaining, acquiesced. Zeckendorf's new thirty-one story building is up but Clinton still does not have the low-rent apartments. A Zeckendorf spokesperson we talked to claims "they just couldn't put their act together. There was so much in-fighting. It was sad."

The other developers who had had visions of hundreds of one-bedroom apartments with hi-fi stereos, bottles of Chardonnay, and upwardly mobile, childless couples arising from the former tenements were stymied. The verdict was in: Clinton would remain substantially as it had been for 100 years.

One last kicker: Clinton got its special district, but the convention center was never built at 47th Street. The City's brush with bankruptcy came in the mid-1970s. All development was put off. When finances recovered, the Jacob Javits Center was constructed down in Chelsea, at 34th Street and Tenth Avenue, instead of at 47th Street.

Trouble Over the Harassment Provision

What galled the speculators and accumulators of land in Clinton most about the new district was the provision in Section 96-109(b) on tenant harassment. As we mentioned above, that provision said that before the Building Department could issue an alteration or demolition permit for a building containing residential uses within the Preservation Area, the Administrator of Housing and Development had to certify "that the eviction and relocation practices followed by the owner of the building satisfy all applicable legal repercussions *and that no harassment has occurred.*"[6] (emphasis added)

Section (b) did not say that the *present* owner had not engaged in harassment, nor that his predecessor as owner had engaged in harassment, nor that no harassment had oc-

curred in the past, say, thirty-six months. The provision drew
no cut-off date. If the Dutch had harassed the Indians in the
seventeenth century, presumably no demolition permit could
be issued.

At least, that is the way Federal District Judge Vincent
L. Broderick interpreted it when the provision was challenged by developers. Part of his 1989 opinion that the provision was unconstitutional stated:

> Under the terms of Section 96-109, the inquiry as to ha-
> rassment may go back to the behavior of the first owner
> of the building, and if by any owner in the chain [there]
> is found to have been harassment, then the restriction
> on all but incidental alterations to the property involved
> operates in perpetuity.
>
> The absence of any limitation...is unreasonable, and
> contrary to due process....
>
> It may very well be that a long moratorium is justifi-
> able and necessary in order to make warehousing by ha-
> rassing landlords unprofitable, but the indefinite exten-
> sion backwards and forwards has no rational basis.
>
> I find that Section 96-109 is unconstitutional on its
> face and represents an undue interference with the use
> of plaintiff's land. It represents an unreasonable regula-
> tion of its use of the land without a rational basis.[7]

Judge Broderick's opinion was never made final because a
settlement was reached and the City amended the offending
harassment section to provide that "no act of harassment
which occurred prior to September 5, 1973 shall constitute harassment for the purposes of this chapter." This amended provision was subsequently upheld by the federal district court.[8]

Evaluation: Clinton in Action

Clinton is the archetype that proves the validity of that
old adage: if you are in doubt about the legality of a municipal law, put it in the zoning code. After all, zoning had been
upheld for almost seventy years—who can successfully
protest? Clinton is a political and social special zoning dis-

trict intended to achieve community ends unrelated to urban design issues. Rent control, tenant selection, mandatory number of rooms—all were intended to preserve a way of life for persons far different from those who reside in the multi-million dollar condos along Fifth Avenue. So far, it appears to be working.

Howard Goldman, a New York attorney whose practice is mostly in environmental law and zoning, offered us one theory to explain Clinton's success:

> Clinton is viable. I think the Clinton special district is an example of one of the more successful districts because it essentially was an anti-development district, and as an anti-development district, it works a hell of a lot better than a district intended to promote development. I think it is easier to regulate development, to put hurdles and obstacles in the path of it, than it is to stimulate it or set out a plan for development to follow. That is what Clinton has done.

Does anyone else agree that the Special Clinton District works? One can get as many different responses to this question as there are persons knowledgeable about the area and the Byzantine world of New York zoning. A sampling of the opinions we heard includes:

> "I have to say that were it not for the existence of the special district, Clinton would have been extinguished or would be on the verge of extinction."

> "Zoning is an imperfect tool for attempting to protect populations from gentrification, and economic change is taking place in Clinton regardless of the zoning restrictions."

> "I would actually give the Clinton district high points. A lot of other people would say low points because it's worked too well. It hasn't been repeated because I think that neighborhood had unique leverage and, boy, were they ever organized."

> "The Clinton district with its objective to temper change is a very successful district because, even though there has been an increase in real estate values and an economic shift in the area (there are more Yuppies moving

in), it has been less dramatic in Clinton than it has been in other areas of the city similarly situated."

"Clinton views [the special district] as one of the more innovative zoning ventures in the City of New York. They see a typewriter being carried up to a second story and they want to know if that violates the special district because it is a commercial or business use."

"There can be no question in anyone's mind that developers are chomping at the bit to get into the district."

"Clinton was one of the most difficult for me to understand. What the City is trying to do is to keep some of those things in business for at least a transitional generation, but I don't know if the Clinton district does it that well."

Change is the one certain event in a metropolis. Demographic changes are often the most profound and noticeable, running through cycles as, first, the white middle class moves outward and the city becomes increasingly divided between the wealthy and the poor. Then the scene shifts again, and the cost of housing in the suburbs and a distaste for its pervading blandness leads young people to move back into the city and refurbish what was a slum building. Patterns of development also change—consider the shifting patterns of growth along Fifth Avenue that we discuss in Chapter 5.

Any regulation that halts change, or at least postpones it, is worth noting. In that respect, we believe that the story of Clinton is a remarkable lesson for other cities. It is a case of preservation, but with a twist. It is historic preservation in the truest sense, without the phoney glitz of the Vieux Carre of New Orleans or the wealth of Beacon Hill in Boston. There is not a single building in Clinton that carries a landmark designation.

The Special Clinton District is used to preserve a neighborhood that provides a living place for the working poor and, for the most, part under conditions that are much the same as they were 100 years ago. And all this is possible in mid-Manhattan, almost surrounded by some of the most expensive real estate in the world.

Fifth Avenue
and Little Italy

The Prince and the Pauper

*Much of the criticism of zoning is true. It works better to
stop or slow some types of development—see Fifth Avenue
—than it does to encourage development—see Little Italy.*

New York Planner

Nothing illustrates the breadth of the special district
phenomenon more than the Special Fifth Avenue District
and the Special Little Italy District. The former is rich, posh,
and the home of multimillionaires; the latter is poor, full of
substandard tenements, and home to Chinese and the descendants of Italian immigrants. The Fifth Avenue district
was hailed as an important innovation; Little Italy left one
ethnic group bitter and many qualified experts dubious as to
its merits.

Special Fifth Avenue District

Background

Fifth Avenue has always occupied a special niche in the
history and lore of American zoning. It was partly because of
pressure by the prestigious Fifth Avenue Association that
zoning was first created in 1916. At that time, the Association was witnessing the expansion of the garment industry

up from Washington Square and east from Seventh Avenue. The merchants did not relish shoppers being pushed off their wide sidewalks by pushcarts full of ladies' and men's clothes. Zoning ensured that commerce and industry would never cross paths on the Avenue again.

The 1916 expansion of the garment industry was only one in a long series of dramatic changes along the Avenue during the nineteenth and twentieth centuries. Fifth Avenue was first sketched out in 1811 by the Commissioners appointed by the State of New York to lay out a "plan for Manhattan." That Commission created New York's grid plan, now so common to American cities. Seymour Toll, noted chronicler of New York's land-use struggles, summarizes the major stages in the Avenue's development in his classic book, *Zoned American*:

> The stretch of the Avenue which begins at Washington Square and courses up the east side of Central Park changed its physical character, its urban function, and its symbolic value through three eras. The first closed during the mid-nineteenth century. The second and third eras bridged the turn of the century....
>
> During the first stage, the Avenue pushed northward through field and marsh, carrying sober, solid homes behind it. The second lined it with a host of examples of what an emergent class of Americans commanded with its new wealth. In the third era, the great houses, hotels, churches, and clubs whose Veblenian style and scale blared out the power and riches of nineteenth-century individuals were remade into works of commerce, shops for the carriage trade, and then a new kind of house for the corporate wealth of the twentieth century.[1]

Since Toll wrote these words, a fourth era has gotten under way, as we shall describe in the next section.

There has been commerce on the Avenue throughout all of its stages. In the early and mid-nineteenth century, commercial buildings and hotels followed the houses as they expanded northward along the Avenue. Gradually, homes were pushed out by retail as it crept north. Following the Civil War, the Vanderbilts, Astors, and Goulds began to build what became known as "Millionaires' Row" from about 60th Street to 70th Street facing Central Park. Posh retail inevitably followed them. A 1975 report by the New School of Social Research summarized the development of the Avenue into a retail boulevard:

> With the opening of DePinna's in 1895, Fifth Avenue became the center of luxury retail activity in the city. In 1902 Franklin and Simon appeared, followed by Tiffany's in 1903 and Altman's in 1906. The establishment of these large retailers encouraged the opening of numerous small shops in the area. The influx of retail establishments onto Fifth Avenue was further accelerated by the end of residential construction along the Avenue. By the late 1920s, most of the mansions along the Avenue had become "white elephants" and were sold cheaply and, for the most part, demolished. Many of these mansions were replaced by such luxury stores as Saks Fifth Avenue and Bergdorf Goodman. It was during these years that Fifth Avenue developed its reputation as one of the nation's finest shopping thoroughfares.[2]

Hotels were brought in to accommodate the tourists who enjoyed the luxury shopping. The Plaza, the Saint Regis, and the Gotham were built between 1901 and 1907. In the Depression era, symbols of the modern office building appeared: the Empire State Building (1931) and Rockefeller Center (1932).

The Problem

In the late 1960s and early 1970s, Fifth Avenue began to enter a fourth stage, one that eventually precipitated the creation of the special district. Rents were escalating. Fancy retail stores such as Best & Co. and DePinna's left the Avenue. (This trend continues today: Altman's has now gone and Bonwit-Teller apparently plans to leave.) New tenants were entering the Avenue: branch banks and airlines, particularly foreign carriers. These offices came to be known as "walk-in billboards." Retailers had to make a profit from their location on the Avenue, but the large Wall Street banks could regard a branch at 55th Street and Fifth Avenue as a promotion—

Airline office, Fifth Avenue.
Photo: *John Babcock*

and charge off part of the exorbitant rent as advertising along the internationally renowned thoroughfare. The foreign airlines, most if not all subsidized by their respective governments, wanted the prestigious locations and did not care how much rent they had to pay. These uses began to crowd out the prime retail that brought so many people to the area in the first place. The Office of Midtown Planning Department (OMPD) reported in 1971 when the district was created that banks and travel agencies (airlines) occupied 21.4 percent of building frontage between 34th and 57th Streets. Retailers occupied only 55 percent of the frontage.[3]

Another threat to the Avenue's retail sector was the office developers. They became aware that the Avenue's department stores and shops were occupying buildings that were not as large as the zoning allowed. The 1975 report by the New School of Social Research noted that:

Previously the Avenue was protected against intensive office development partly because of difficulties in land assemblage and high property values....The effectiveness of these deterrents diminished as the number of office building sites elsewhere declined. Furthermore, most of Fifth Avenue was not developed to its full zoned potential. A study conducted by the OMPD entitled "The Impact of the Fifth Avenue Special District Legislation on Retail Floor Space on Fifth Avenue" identified twenty "soft sites" along Fifth Avenue which possibly could be redeveloped during the 1970s and 1980s. These sites contained 24 percent (1.68 million square feet) of the special district's approximately 7 million square feet of retail space. It was further projected that if these sites were in fact redeveloped under the old zoning regulation (C5-3), the Avenue would suffer a net loss of 1.389 million square feet of retail space. The assessed value of the land was between four and five times higher than the value of the four- to twelve-story structures built on it.[4]

The threat was clear: Fifth Avenue could, if nothing were done, become as sterile as Sixth Avenue with its glass-walled imitations of Mies Van der Rohe. The world's most famous shopping street was up for sale.

The Special District

Donald Elliott was Chairman of the Planning Commission in 1971. He told us that the purpose of the Fifth Avenue Special District was to achieve two goals: stop the influx of banks and airline offices and encourage residential uses above the stores. When the planning staff suggested adding residential to commercial uses, they were hardly picturing the traditional market street with *paisans* dancing in dirndle dresses outside of their bakery/apartments. Their vision ran more along the lines of expensive condos in buildings like Trump Tower—just enough housing to bring some life to the Avenue after 6:00 p.m. Elliott explained the reasoning behind this:

Fifth Avenue really came from a fairly simple proposition, which was that it has traditionally been the great

department store street. Those high-end department
stores, again, are part of this network of the city and
their concentration is useful. And it was pretty clear
that we're again dealing with an institution that was not
in the forefront of growth, and these stores were beginning to be cut back, and the land was becoming so valuable that it seemed to us pretty likely that Fifth Avenue
would become just simply another office street which,
while there is nothing wrong with that generally, when
you put it in the context of the rest of the city, it just was
one step to eliminate the diversity that makes the city
great in our judgment. So we wanted to figure out a way
to encourage the continuation and, in fact, the replacement of these large stores.

Elliott went on to say that the planners decided that the
best way to make the sites along Fifth Avenue more valuable
was to allow residential units above the stores. According to
Elliott, "We also believed that the strict division between
commercial and residential development was really a mistake and that the mixed-use city, which is typified at least in
part by Paris and London, is really a more sensible development." The slight additional density that would be added by
putting residential units above the shops did not worry the
Planning Commission because the Avenue was very wide.
Mixing uses would have the added advantage of spreading
the peak of demand for lighting and heating.

Elliott gave us an interesting insight into the process of
creating a special district from the planning staff's point of view:

There is always a question of how far you go with this
regulatory business. You've got to be very careful not to
go too far. There is an enormous temptation. It is so easy
to think that in your enthusiasm and good motivation
that somehow you know more than you do. When you get
designers in the Department of City Planning who are
being paid $15,000 a year telling the great design archi-
tects of the world how a building ought to look, I back
off. I say that's crazy. The key, as we saw it, was to try to
identify, if you could, the things that were really important and lay down some rules about them and then try
to get out of the way of the rest.

So that is what they tried to do. On March 26, 1971, the Special Fifth Avenue District was recommended by the Planning Commission. The district was to stretch from 58th to 38th Streets and extend 200 feet back on the east and west sides of the Avenue.

The OMPD set out the basic rationale for the district in the Planning Commission's recommendation to the Board of Estimate:

1. Comparative luxury shopping facilities must be in Midtown in order to maintain the city's economic strength and environmental desirability;
2. Fifth Avenue is the best location for these facilities;
3. Comparative luxury shopping requires large department stores and/or major specialty shops;
4. The disappearance, in recent years, of certain major specialty shops threatens the continued viability of retailing on the Avenue;
5. The major problem of these stores is the "push" from office development;
6. Government intervention is the only means to restore the Avenue's retailing strength; and
7. The granting of inducements to developers is the best method of intervention.[5]

The support was almost unanimous. The Real Estate Board of New York, the Fifth Avenue Association, the Citizen Housing and Planning Council, the Municipal Art Society, and the *New York Times* all endorsed the concept.

The district regulations* were not particularly revolutionary, but they did represent governmental interference with market forces—if one regards branch banks and subsidized airline offices as part of the natural market. The ground floors of buildings facing the Avenue are limited in the future to certain listed uses, mostly retail or restaurant (see Appendix C). The regulations ensured that retail would remain close to street level by requiring that "retail or service establishments shall be located on levels up to but not exceeding a height of six stories or eighty-five feet, whichev-

*When the Special Midtown District was adopted in 1982, Fifth Avenue became a special subdistrict with substantially the same regulations.

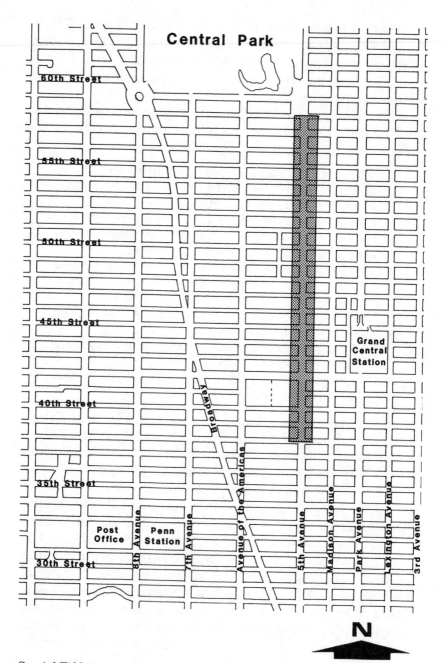

Special Fifth Avenue District.
Source: *New York City Planning Commission*

er is less, or not more than five feet below curb level."[6] Branch banks and airline offices cannot occupy more than 15 percent of the linear street frontage.

In order to try to preserve what planners perceived as the traditional ambience of the Avenue, signs are restricted to no more than one-third of the window area, and banners or pennants on the exterior of buildings are forbidden. Setbacks along Fifth Avenue are prohibited for the first eighty-five feet of height. Hotel, office, and apartment lobbies are not permitted on the Avenue unless the building is inaccessible from another street. No off-street parking facilities are permitted within the special subdistrict. Residential use is allowed on upper stories along the Avenue, and developers can get additional FAR for building residential units.

Perhaps the most successful of the developments under the special subdistrict is the Trump Tower at 56th Street. At least, it is successful in the monetary sense, perhaps less so aesthetically, unless one is inclined to gloss and brass, a piano player pounding away in the lobby, and a waterfall cascading down the atrium as the escalators carry eager shoppers up and down the first six stories. Above the sixth floor are very expensive condominiums. Trump Tower made use of all the bonuses offered under the new special subdistrict and ended up with an FAR of 21.

Evaluation

Of course, the City did nothing to affect the existing institutional uses along the Avenue. Air France—a nonconforming use—can be occupied by El Al; a branch of Manufacturers Trust can give way to one of Citicorp. The District put a stop to a new trend; it did not reverse it.

Simply trying to stop the market trend was a rather nervy thing to do. The special district was a clear political intervention in the market forces working on perhaps the most ostentatious commercial area in the world. Yet, the planning staff reassured itself by the belief that what was happening to the Avenue was not really due to market forces at all, but to subsidies with which many fancy stores could not compete. Elliott reported:

> This business of store uses walked pretty close to the edge of meddling, but we were determined to try to have Fifth Avenue not turn into Sixth Avenue. That was sort of the rallying cry.

Towards this end, the staff has encouraged developers to put in housing along the Avenue. Although none of them have been quite as successful as the Trump Tower, they hope that the cumulative effect will be an atmosphere more closely resembling that of Paris or London.

This effort probably would not work in most smaller American cities where "downtown" does not have so much appeal, and commuting to and from the suburbs is not so difficult. But cities such as Chicago, San Francisco, Philadelphia, and Los Angeles have tried the mixed-use concept with some success.

Special Little Italy District

If Fifth Avenue is a good example of the success a special district can achieve when it has the approbation of the entire community, Little Italy is a case study of the pitfalls a district can encounter if it does not have full community support.

Background

Little Italy lies near the southern tip of Manhattan. First occupied by the Irish, the area was settled in the early 1900s by many Italian immigrants who soon became the predominant resident group, somewhat akin to Boston's North End. However, Little Italy lies just north of Chinatown, and in the past thirty years many Chinese have moved into the district.

A 1975 New School of Social Research report comparing census data from 1960 and 1970 illustrated the steady erosion of Italian presence in the district:

Little Italy is 57.3 percent white (1960: 87.2 percent), 38.4 percent Chinese (1960: 11.5 percent), and 4 percent black (1960: 1.2 percent). The ethnic composition shows a community that has undergone radical changes in its makeup but one that has remained fairly stable in size. Those of foreign stock are 73.3 percent (1960: 57.6 percent). Italians account for 30.1 percent (1960: 69.1 percent), Chinese contribute 38 percent (1960: 12 percent), while South and Central Americans add 11 percent.[7]

The report also noted that the relatively low number of children and old people living in the area seemed to indicate that families left the area if they could afford to do so. The remaining inhabitants lived in dilapidated Old Law tenements; no new housing had been built for over sixty years. The area was peppered with scores of dreary shops and small manufacturing plants. By the early 1970s, Little Italy was poor, deteriorating, and not very Italian anymore.

Educating the Community

In the mid-1970s, the idea of doing something with this depressed area caught on with City Planning staff. There is some disagreement over where exactly the idea for a Little Italy special district originated. Some believe it started with the formation of the Little Italy Restoration Association (LIRA) in 1974 to underscore the Italian presence and resist the Chinese influx; others say it was the idea of the Planning Commission when John Zuccotti was Chairman. No one can discount the importance of the Italian residents who formed LIRA, persons like Messrs. Vitale and Graddi, undertakers; Mr. Ianello, then owner of Umberto's Clam House; Anna Capparelli, a sixth-generation resident of Little Italy; Frank Russo, the Democratic district leader; and Father Maranacchi, representing parishes in the area.

Raquel Ramati and Patrick Ping-Tze Too were the planning staff members in charge of Little Italy. Their principal focus was on Mulberry Street, the spine of the area. Mulberry Street is a bustling, six-block cluster of restaurants and specialty shops selling imported food and gifts. It is the

Mulberry Street, looking south, Special Little Italy District.
Photo: *John Babcock*

most festive place in the district, chock-full of family-owned
restaurants with tables on the sidewalks and the center of
various festivities, headed by the *festa* of San Gennaro, the
patron saint of Naples. Busy as it was, the street reflected
the general deterioration of the neighborhood and had become rather shabby.

Ramati, Too, and others on the staff worked late hours
preparing colored drawings to illustrate to the community the
types of things that could be done to improve the appearance
of Mulberry Street. Selling these ideas to the Italian residents
was a formidable task. In Chapter 2 of her book, *How to Save
Your Own Street*, Ramati describes the process:

> It is hard to define how one creates a sense of partnership
> and participation between government and the commu-
> nity. How does one explain complex and sometimes dry
> concepts to a group that faces government with a sense of
> skepticism and suspicion, and convince them that the pro-

fessional is not an elitist with a sense of superiority? Anyone who wants a clear answer may find no one single reliable answer. But the day the architects presented the community with these realistic drawings of the street, the trust surfaced and the dialogue began. It was the first time that the local people saw vividly what their street looked like in its totality. It gave them a sense of pride. The clean and beautiful line drawings allowed the imagination of everyone to flow and envision how they, too, could change and improve their own environment.[8]

All of this public education paid off. The prominent Italian residents and businesses became enthusiastic about the possibility of a special district.

The Special Little Italy District

In early 1977, the Special Little Italy District was approved by the Planning Commission and adopted by the Board of Estimate. As we shall discuss in the next section, the ordinance passed in the face of considerable opposition, particularly from representatives of the Chinese community.

The Special Little Italy District is bounded on the south by Canal Street and on the north by Bleeker Street (one block north of Houston Street). The western boundary starts north along Baxter Street, jogs west to follow Center Street and Lafayette Street, and then cuts back east to run up Mulberry Street. The eastern boundary is the heavily travelled Bowery Street from Canal to Bleeker.

The district is divided into four subdistricts, but the true focus is the Mulberry Street Regional Spine. Except for the block north of Houston Street, the district limits building heights to six stories in keeping with the existing scale of the area. Along Mulberry Street, the district guidelines mandate "transparency" on the ground floor. "[This] means," Ramati wrote, "opening the ground level with doors or windows, in order to prevent blank walls along the street and to enhance the pedestrian streets."[9] In keeping with this idea, the permitted uses along Mulberry Street are the dozens of retail uses that are usually found in any neighborhood business zone.

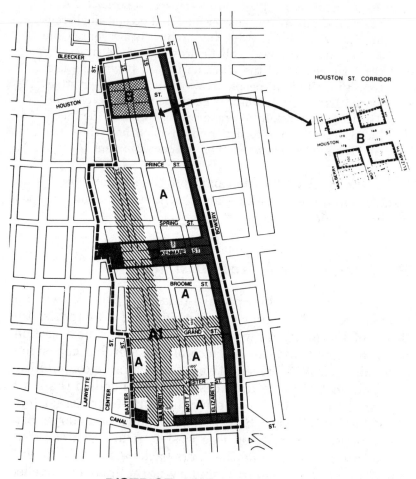

DISTRICT MAP

A	☐	PRESERVATION AREA
A1	▨	MULBERRY ST. REGIONAL SPINE
B	▩	HOUSTON ST. CORRIDOR
C	■	BOWERY, CANAL, KENMARE ST.
---		DISTRICT BOUNDARY

Special Little Italy District.
Source: *New York City Planning Commission*

There are other provisions and subdistricts meant to guide and encourage new development, although little has occurred thus far. Outside of Mulberry Street, most of the rest of the district is designated as a Preservation Area. There is a short stretch along the Houston Street corridor where taller and bulkier buildings are permitted; the Bowery is a subdistrict where manufacturing and truck traffic is encouraged. The Commission also hoped to create a park west of Mulberry Street by giving developers an FAR bonus if they would contribute to a fund, but this failed to materialize.

Opposition to the District

It is ironic that the very community outreach that enabled the staff to sell the district idea to one segment of the area's residents probably served to further alienate the rest. As we intimated earlier, not all residents of the area were happy about this district. The following appears in the minutes at the Planning Commission hearing before the district was approved:

> Speakers opposed to the proposed amendments included the Chairman of the Chinese Consolidated Benevolent Association, a member of the New York City Commission on Human Rights, a representative of the Chinatown Improvement Council, a representative of Asian Americans for Equal Employment, a member of the New York City Art Commission, the Chairman of the Chinese Import and Export Association of America, and several residents of the community. Community Planning Board No. 2 requested that the amendments be withdrawn without prejudice for further discussion. The hearing was closed.[10]

The Chinese felt that the new district was a not-so-subtle device to keep them out. Indeed, some observers say that when LIRA first went to the Commission with their request that something be done about the area, they expressed anger and concern over the influx of Chinese. Some members of the staff claim that they in turn told the LIRA repre-

sentatives that they would do nothing to exclude one particular ethnic group; they could only help with the *physical*
restoration of the area.

Doris Deither, neither Italian nor Chinese, who was
then head of the Zoning Committee of Community Board No.
2. told us a slightly different story of the events that led to
the district's adoption:

DD   The Community Board had no input whatever.
     The liaison to the City Planning Commission who
     was supposedly working with our Board on all the
     issues had been working with the community
     down there on the Little Italy proposal [but] had
     never brought it to us although she came to all our
     meetings....We wanted a liaison who was going to
     be working with the Community Board like [she
     was] supposed to. So she lost her job on that....So
     then we started meeting with the [Italian] commu-
     nity down there. They already had been told ev-
     erything was fine. They didn't even want to dis-
     cuss it. We wanted to ask some questions about
     this. I tried to get across to them some of the prob-
     lems I saw in the district, and they weren't inter-
     ested. We also sought a meeting with the Chinese,
     which got them very upset. I insisted that, since
     this was a community plan, all the community
     people had to be involved. So we contacted a num-
     ber of the Chinese organizations and we had them
     to meetings. We had five Italians and five Chinese,
     I guess, and me and Ramati, and that was when
     we started clashing because the Chinese didn't
     want to talk in front of the Italians, and so I had a
     meeting with the Italians, and I had a meeting
     with the Chinese.
RFB Like a labor negotiation.
DD   [Ramati] was furious that I had a meeting with
     the Chinese.

The Chinese in Little Italy are by no means a homoge-
nous community. There are old and young, radicals, liberals,
conservatives, Communists, and even a few Republicans. But
all of these groups became angry activists when their position

in the community was threatened. On one occasion while the special district regulations were still being drafted, the City proposed to tear down some loft buildings that housed substandard dwellings. Community Board No. 2 put out notices of a public meeting on the proposal. Deither told us:

> They have about seven or eight Chinese newspapers down there. The Chinese unions got involved. They brought 500 people to my meeting. All of them with signs. We had to have a Chinese interpreter. They brought 500 people out to oppose the parking garage on the site of the buildings because, apparently, the City doesn't do [its] homework. If they had checked those local buildings, they would know that... [on] every floor in those loft buildings were garment workers, Chinese garment workers. So the union came out....The City gave up. We heard some of the people from the Chinese community were nervous about this parking garage, and so they came down to the meeting thinking that there would be nobody there and they could come down and protest the parking garage. They walked in, and they couldn't even find a seat. We had standing room only that night. All the seats were taken within fifteen minutes of the time the meeting was due to start.

One of the problems with the Special Little Italy District was that the City never did do its homework in the Chinese community. Thus, a district was created that seemed to exclude the majority of its residents.

Norman Marcus explained his doubts about the appropriateness of the district:

> There are many districts that are meaningless. The Little Italy district was. From the standpoint of what happened: very little or nothing. From the psychological standpoint, it was a plus....It raised the consciousness of that [Italian] community, which was in need of consciousness raising because they were rapidly being engulfed by the Chinese. It then paradoxically turned into a disaster because they published a book—a little brochure on the Little Italy Special District—and did a three-color process on the cover with an Italian flag.... The book got into the hands of one of the Chinese com-

munity leaders, and they threatened to march on City Hall from Chinatown because, actually, most of Little Italy was owned and occupied by the Chinese except for the restaurants on Mulberry Street. That ultimately—typical Planning Commission politics—led to a special district for Chinatown [Manhattan Bridge Special District, adopted on August 20, 1981]....We said we'll leave the Little Italy on the books, but we'll do a Chinatown special district that you'll like even more.

Evaluation

Was the Little Italy Special District really necessary? According to Michael Parley, who was part of the Urban Design Group from 1972-1981, "Little Italy district, at the time it was developed, was something of a fiction because it was a district designed to guide development where we didn't believe there would be any development. It was more a public relations special district than it was an actual zoning and urban design district." On the other hand, Patrick Too, the architect of many of the concepts in the district, believes that "there is a certain merit in that particular district, although today you can see the same guidelines in many, many zones, in many, many of our areas."

It is true that there has been very little new residential development in the area since the special district was created. It still has practically no open space. A provision to give builders an FAR bonus if they would contribute to a fund for a second park has never been used.

The special district did stimulate a dozen or so new restaurants on Mulberry Street. Today, one can say that Mulberry Street is a success, if success is measured by the number of tourists who troop through it and pause to have an espresso or cappucino at a sidewalk cafe. But the true accomplishment of the district is that it gave one segment of its population a renewed pride—"I live in Little Italy." For this reason, the district will probably never be removed from the books.

Conclusion

Both Fifth Avenue and Little Italy illustrate the strengths and weaknesses of special zoning. In particular, they demonstrate how important it is to have strong community support for the zoning change. Their experience also may suggest that it is easier to stop economic change than to stimulate it. And even special districts do not seem to be able to stop change at all, especially social change, if it has already gone too far.

Special zoning on Fifth Avenue seems to have stopped some types of economic development there; it did put a stop to changes that were not consistent with the character (or image) of the Avenue. This successful district had almost unanimous support from various citizen groups. On the other hand, the Little Italy special district did not have unanimous support. Resistance to economic growth played no part in Little Italy's story as it did in Fifth Avenue (and Clinton), and since then, no new development has taken place beyond the refurbishing of Mulberry Street. Changes there seem to have passed the point of no return before the district was created, and there is no evidence that its existence has slowed down the influx of Chinese.

Midtown

Strangling
the Golden Goose

The East Side was getting intolerable, had become intolerable.

Joseph Rose, Director, Community Board No. 5

One has to be mad, crippled, or a first-time tourist to take a cab cross-town on the East Side of mid-Manhattan; a lame and blind cow could make better time. Even though the streets—or most of them—are one-way, double-parking of hosts of delivery trucks usually means that one lane only is "open," and that only in a figurative sense.

From Sixth Avenue to Second Avenue—seven blocks—it is as though one has entered a canyon of glass and cement interrupted only by bleak and mostly uninhabitable plazas, the curse of the 1961 revised zoning ordinance. Even those who live in Manhattan, particularly the movers and shakers, had long known that something had to be done.

The Canyonization
of Mid-Manhattan

New York City's 1960s building boom had undergone a painful decline in the 1970s, but it roared ahead in the latter part of the decade and the early 1980s, fueled, in part, by the encouragement of the Koch administration. Most of this new construction took place on the East Side of mid-

Manhattan north of 42nd Street and south of 59th Street.
As Manhattan entered into its post-industrial era, manufacturing and blue-collar jobs gave way to service industries,
insurance companies, and advertising agencies; even law offices and accountants moved north from their ancient do-
main in lower Manhattan.

Large new office buildings for these businesses were
jackknifed into small parcels as developers milked every
bonus made available by the 1961 ordinance. Among other
bonuses, the concept of the "zoning lot" allowed builders to
merge the allowable FAR of one tax lot with that of a contiguous tax lot and build even higher.

Opportunity Zoning

Predictability and certainty, as originally set out in the
1916 ordinance, had disappeared under the 1961 revisions.
Almost every new building was constructed through a special
permit, exception, text change, or variance. The process more
resembled a Middle Eastern bazaar than the government of
the world's most prestigious city. And it seemed as if each
new building was bigger than the one before.

Michael Kwartler, who was with the City Planning
Commission from 1967 to 1976, described the condition of
zoning in Midtown in the years preceding the adoption of the
special district in 1982:

> When we did the research for the Midtown zoning, no
> one was sure who the culprit was, who was giving away
> the kitchen sink, although it seemed to people on the
> street that someone was giving it away. City Planning
> [CPC] thought it was the Board of Standards and Ap-
> peals [BSA]. So we researched every special permit, both
> from the BSA and CPC for the history of the 1961 zoning
> ordinance, and found out that it was really City Plan-
> ning that was giving away the kitchen sink because they
> could write legislation [through special permits]. All that
> BSA could do was give you a little bit here and there on
> specific hardship. Their stuff was negligible.

According to Kwartler, a major culprit was Section 7475 of the 1961 zoning ordinance, which allowed the Planning Commission to waive other zoning restrictions for Midtown lots over a certain size if the proposed project had what the Commission considered "good design." This section essentially gave Midtown a "floating zone" for exceptions. Kwartler continued:

> It got to the point by the mid-1970s [that] there were no as-of-right buildings being built in Midtown. Every building was being negotiated and [Section 7475] effectively was the zoning ordinance. IBM, AT&T, Trump Tower, One Park Plaza, virtually every building, in fact every building, in Midtown was going for a special permit because of what the special permit process allowed you to do....
>
> I can tell you which buildings were built at each point and Norman [Marcus] would then generalize it so it didn't look as though it was spot zoning. But for all intents and purposes, these were modified every time a developer came in with a proposal. It's what I would call "opportunity zoning" or opportunity planning. And there were virtually no criteria. AT&T was a confusion between architecture and urban design at its worst. AT&T is the point at which everybody got blinded. Planning Commission and staff loved [that] building. And maybe it's a nice building, and maybe it isn't. That's another discussion. But they were willing to waive everything. That building set back daylighting to pre-1916 standards. That is what I would call a streetwall with a vengeance. And IBM, AT&T, Trump Tower are all examples of buildings [that] pushed that idea really to the limit.

And the developers held most of the cards. When such world-renowned architects as Phillip Johnson and Edward Barnes put their names on drawings for a high rise, the underpaid planning staff were hard put to reject their ideas.

For the period from 1977 (when the boom recommenced) to 1982 (when the special district was created) only thirteen out of thirty-four buildings were approved as-of-right. The Midtown area was becoming a corporate office park, soon to be devoid of residential development.

Demands for Reform

Alex Garvin, from 1970 to 1974 Director of Housing and Community Development for the Planning Commission, explained how this frenetic activity led to demands for a change:

> AG   [The Planning Commission] had no criteria for evaluating daylight impact or sunlight. No criteria for wind effects. Around the AT&T building is a disaster area in the winter. There are no setbacks to break the wind and (given the sheer size of it) IBM is actually worse because its skin is so smooth. But for all intents and purposes, they are very similar. Everybody was just enamored of the building. And then, the object of having this Section 7475 was then they could fine tune each building to the next building. Well, here's really the rub. IBM, AT&T, and Trump Tower were actually all being planned simultaneously, and I ask you, why is the conservatory of the IBM Building in perpetual shadow? Because of the shadow from AT&T....Actually that particular special permit is what shaped Midtown more so than any of the special districts, interestingly enough. That was the tail that wagged the dog for about five years. The developers actually became dissatisfied with it because, as the public clamor increased, particularly after those buildings were virtually completed or people began to visualize that, light and air became an issue in New York and what is being given away here.
>
> RFB Is that clamor that you spoke of what probably led to the Midtown revision?
>
> AG   Yes. It did lead to that. It certainly wasn't from the architects. They were having a ball.

The good government types finally had had enough; Midtown residents began to put pressure on City Hall to slow growth on the East Side of Midtown and to put back some certainty into the permitting process instead of the negotiation that had come to characterize it. Even the developers began to tire of the game. They were never sure just what would be permitted for each project. Such prestigious organizations as the Park Council, the Regional Plan Association, the Landmarks Conservancy, and the New York Chapters of the American Institute of Architects, American Planning Association, and American Society of Landscape Architects, all demanded a change.

The Special Midtown District

Work began on the new special district in 1979. The Planning Commission had four goals:

1. Slow growth on the East Side of mid-Manhattan;
2. Encourage development on the west and south sides (where little had occurred thus far);
3. Provide more as-of-right development; and
4. Encourage more residential development in the midblock areas between the avenues.

These ambitions directly challenged "natural" market forces. Nevertheless, the regulations were adopted on May 13, 1982, after more than 200 meetings with a wide variety of interest groups. With few exceptions, the new special district was acclaimed by all.

The regulations for the new special district were listed in a 276-page report entitled "Midtown Zoning" that was issued on the same day the district was adopted. The district was divided into Growth, Stabilization, and Preservation Areas "to serve as a framework for public policy and zoning decisions." The report described the three areas as follows:

1. In the West Side Growth Area, bounded by Sixth to Eighth Avenues from 40th to 60th Streets, density on Sixth Avenue, Seventh Avenue, and Broadway is increased from a floor area ratio of 15 times the lot area to a floor area ratio (FAR) of 18 times (FAR 18), subject to a six-year sunset clause. The maximum density is not increased above the present FAR 21.6. Midblocks remain at FAR 15.
2. In the East Side Stabilization Area, bounded by Sixth to Third Avenues from 40th to 60th Streets, densities

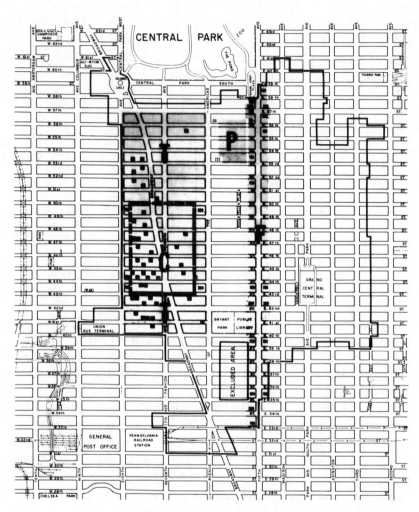

MIDTOWN DISTRICT PLAN
MAP I - SPECIAL MIDTOWN DISTRICT AND SUB DISTRICTS

- F FIFTH AVENUE SUB DISTRICT
- T THEATRE SUB DISTRICT
- P PRESERVATION SUB DISTRICT
- ▓ THEATRE SUB DISTRICT CORE
- ■ LISTED THEATRES

Special Midtown District, with Subdistricts.
Source: *New York City Planning Commission*

would be reduced. The majority of sites could not exceed FAR 15-16 on the avenues and FAR 12-13 in the midblocks. At present, most buildings can reach FAR 18 throughout Midtown and FAR 21.6 in the Special Fifth Avenue District.

3. In the Midblock Preservation Area, between Sixth and Fifth Avenues from the north side of 53rd Street to the north side of 56th Street, density is reduced from FAR 10-12 to FAR 8 to retain the character, scale, and function of this area.[1]

In other words, the West Side was given ample room to grow, while the East Side and midblocks were held in check. As we have mentioned in previous chapters, the new Midtown district also incorporated the old Theater and Fifth Avenue special districts as special subdistricts.

The new regulations made substantive changes. In order to discourage more growth, bonusable amenities were sharply reduced on the East Side of Midtown. The 1961 bonus for plazas was reduced from FAR 3 to FAR 1. No combination of bonuses could increase the base FAR by more than 20 percent. The midblocks between the avenues were reduced to lower FARs than the properties on the avenues. In the Preservation Area (from 53rd to 56th Streets and from Fifth Avenue to Sixth Avenue, near the Museum of Modern Art), the FAR was reduced from 12 to 8 except for the section within 150 feet of the avenues. New buildings would be required without bonus to provide additional pedestrian circulation space at ground level in proportion to the building's floor area, maintain streetwall and retail continuity on designated avenues and streets, and relocate adjacent subway stairs from the public sidewalk to the development lot.

Probably the most important element meant to encourage development was the increase in the FAR to 18 on the West Side of the district. The kicker was the sunset clause on the increase, requiring the new FAR 18 to revert back to FAR 15 in 1988. Even on the West Side, the City was not going to allow a building boom to proceed indefinitely.

An immediate problem in implementing the district was the extreme complexity of these regulations. If the provisions in the other districts were complex, the provisions in the Midtown district were Sanskrit. Even the planners knew this. The regulations were so complex that the planners provided the text of the regulations in the Midtown Zoning report with a running marginal translation that is labeled "Plain English!"

Raquel Ramati, one of Lindsay's original "red squad" of urban designers, commented on the package of Midtown regulations:

> But I think that it also is very inflexible. Very, very inflexible on some of the points. Too inflexible. It is true it is easier to enforce. Maybe. It's not real easy to enforce because people are making money just by trying to understand the formula of the Midtown zoning. It is so complicated that some people just make money understanding the formula which, I think, is ridiculous. So I don't think it is that simple.

Nevertheless, the Midtown Zoning report optimistically predicted: "The cumulative effect of the above proposals would go a long way toward eliminating negotiated zoning. They would permit development to proceed on a more predictable and as of-right basis."[2]

Opinions

Has it worked? One can find as many different answers as there are experts. Alex Garvin told us:

> From a planning point of view, it makes real sense. You have the Eighth Avenue subway [on the West Side], which is underutilized at a time when the Second Avenue line was not built and Lexington Avenue is way overloaded. You would have less displacement. I think the notion of moving development westward is a legitimate planning objective. I'm not sure that you need a special district to achieve that. If anybody had any courage, what they would do is downzone the theaters to a floor area ratio where they couldn't be built on and upzone Eighth Avenue to the maximum possible. The smut would disap-

pear pretty damn fast and the developers would gobble up that stuff and that would be the end of it.

Michael Kwartler was more positive:

There is a lot more as-of-right development in Midtown. Have a look at the numbers. At least half of the new buildings that have been built under the new Midtown regulations have been as-of-right buildings.

And most developers would prefer that they would be—they are actually willing to settle for less and have the certainty that they can proceed, that they know there is a market and that they can somehow meet that market because it's a more predictable time schedule....We're doing one now in Times Square where the developer actually could have picked up more development rights if he'd gotten involved with the theaters and so on and other bonuses and gallerias and played it all through. [But] first of all, it's a year tacked on to the process while you are sitting on the land, and at these prices, that could make or break a project, although some of them are quite clever at never closing. It's amazing. I just get a kind of practical glimpse of what goes on, but these guys must have stomachs of steel the way they continue to play this out without flinching.

We had the following exchange with John Zuccotti, who seemed to feel that the new regulations are too complicated:

JZ   Under these new regulations, they talk about as-of-right solutions, right? Only a few people can figure out what the as-of-right solution is. So we now have work, not just to process, but just to figure out how to...

RFB You're talking about Midtown?

JZ   I'm talking about specifically on the Midtown question.

RFB Their great theme is they want to take out this discretion and make it...

JZ   I know that that's the theme, but I don't see it happening that way.

On the other hand, Sandy Hornick of the current planning staff responded: "I think Midtown was successful in its primary objective to steer development to the west and to encourage as-of-right development rather than by special permits. I think those two things worked reasonably well."

The Planning Commission certainly believes the district has worked well. In July, 1987, the Commission published a sixteen-page pamphlet entitled *Midtown Development Review*. That booklet is enthusiastic—to put it modestly—about the results: growth on the West Side has been significant; more as-of-right buildings have been processed; more mixed-use development—residential, office, and retail—has occurred. The canyonization east of Fifth Avenue has been halted.

The report summarized the achievements of the Special Midtown District:

> Many of the key goals set out in the 1981 Midtown Development Report are being achieved. Growth has been shifted from the East to the West Sides of Midtown—8.3 million square feet of privately developed space has been approved west of Sixth Avenue, compared with the 5.9 million square feet approved east of Sixth Avenue. ("Approved" buildings in this report are those which have been granted a special permit by the Board of Estimate or issued a building permit by the Department of Buildings.) Many new buildings provide retail stores or pedestrian amenities such as added sidewalk space. One-third of all the new buildings contain residential units, enriching this predominantly commercial district. New buildings display a variety of architectural forms while protecting light and air. At the same time, new regulations which allow flexibility within performance standards have permitted the vast majority of development (80 percent of new buildings) to proceed as-of-right, a sharp change from the negotiated zoning which had become commonplace prior to the district.[3]

Continued Violations

Even with this apparent reform, negotiation by developers goes on, and developers continue to violate the zoning laws in the belief they can then bargain with the City for a variance to legalize the violation.

In the April 10, 1989, issue of *New York* magazine, John Taylor published an article entitled "Pushing the Outer Limits." In this article, Taylor describes the experience of builder Harry Macklowe and his new hotel on West 44th Street. It seems that Macklowe had hired a contractor to demolish some old buildings on the site that allegedly were Single Room Occupancy (SRO) hotels. While Macklowe was out of town, the contractor came in one night and, by the next morning, the buildings were leveled. SROs are a big issue in New York City because they are housing for the poor and are being demolished all over the city. The Macklowe event occurred two days before a moratorium went into effect on the destruction or conversion of SROs. The outcry was furious— every politician showed up to have his or her photo taken before the hotel. The City sued and Macklowe paid a $2 million fine, a pittance for most large builders. Taylor quotes Ruth Messinger, a City Council member, as saying: "All this does is send a signal that justice is for sale in New York, that you can break the law with impunity as long as you are willing to surrender some of your profit to the mayor."[4]

A similar remark was attributed by Taylor to Harrison Golden, City Comptroller: "We have a city where the message has been sent out that zoning restrictions are to be flouted. The appropriate public policies should be to establish limits on excursions in light, air, and space. Now they are points of departure for negotiations. It's like buying indulgences in the Middle Ages."

Taylor continued on to relate how, at 156 West 56th Street (also in the Midtown Special District), a building known as Cityspire was built under a special permit authorizing a seventy-story structure. This tower was almost twice the height of the original zoning. When the building went up, it turned out to be fourteen feet higher than authorized by the special permit. The builder, Bruce Eichner, applied for a change in the permit and was turned down by the Planning Commission. Eichner, according to Taylor, sued the City and kept right on building. A deal was struck. Eichner could keep his fourteen feet. In return, he would build 7,200 feet of dance/rehearsal space above an adjacent arcade. "A lawsuit is often merely a precursor to a settlement," Taylor observes, "and such was the case with Cityspire. The City Planning Commission approved this deal, as did the Board of Estimate late last week." The Mayor did force Eichner to dismantle the dome on the top of Cityspire.

Joseph Rose, head of Community Board No. 5, is quoted by Taylor: "There's a lot of shady dealing in New York real estate. It's hard enough keeping people straight. But if you treat [the fines levied for breaking the law] as a cost of doing business, then marginal behavior becomes acceptable. Then you have the outlaw developer syndrome...City Hall is now acting as an ombudsman for this kind of real-estate developer."

So the portrait of the Special Midtown District's success is not as rosy as is painted by the Planning Commission. Yet, Koch's allies point out that his policies brought prosperity to the City, and that the critics are complaining about exactly the policies that turned around the economic condition of the metropolis. This position implies that good planning is inimical to financial well-being.

Conclusion

What is the lesson from this major rezoning in Midtown Manhattan for other large cities? We suspect that most major urban areas that are not engaged in some type of "slow growth" effort will actually wish they had Manhattan's problems.

But the Midtown experience is an important warning of what can happen when growth runs wild. In mid-Manhattan, all zoning had become a matter of negotiation, something like bargaining in the souks. If a blatant violation occurred, the developers realized they could bargain and settle the dispute by purchase of the violation—in effect, by sharing a portion of their profits with the City.

The Special Midtown District represents an effort to shift growth from one place in the city to another. It has achieved moderate success in this by putting barriers in the way of big projects on the East Side and by removing barriers on the West. Its success in regularizing the permit process is more problematic. The new district has, to some extent, cut down the unprincipled haggling. Growth to the east of Sixth Avenue seems to have slowed, and it is true that more development now takes place according to the district's specific regulations. On the other hand, outrageous violations still occur.

The attempt to stimulate growth west of Sixth Avenue by offering a five-year increase in the FAR may have worked better. New development, indeed, has taken place in that area. It is too early to tell what this new growth will mean for Clinton or for the now largely abandoned waterfront: proposals are on the boards for large-scale private development along the Hudson River. We probably have not heard the last of Donald Trump's proposal for a gargantuan project on the Upper West Side west of 11th Street. If current proposals for commercial and residential towers along the Hudson River move along under the new administration, it will be the final icing on the canyonization of Manhattan.

Garment Center

A Stitch In Time?

If it works, it would be the kind of situation in which to do a special district.
                    Sandy Hornick, Director, Zoning Study Group,
                              New York City Planning Commission

So what you've got is Calvin Klein and his accountants and publicity people and sales people who count in the census of manufacturing orders, but the people who are actually cutting the pants and sewing the pockets on them are not in the garment center anymore.
                         Arthur Margon, Executive Director,
                              Real Estate Board of New York City

What should not be ignored...is that these activities in the Garment Center, in terms of business establishment, employment, occupied space and volume of business, [are] critical to the economic well-being of New York City and State.
                              New York Appellate Court, May 1990

The City of New York has not confined the "benefits" of special districts to ethnic neighborhoods nor "sexy" areas such as theater districts and upscale retail boulevards. The City also uses the technique to preserve and protect less glamorous areas that are threatened by social and economic pressure. Most major cities still have older manufacturing and industrial areas that are regarded as community assets—notwithstanding their less than pleasing aromas, noises, and vistas—because of the jobs they provide. Unfortunately, these areas generally face substantial pressure to convert to non-manufacturing uses usually more profitable to the property owner, as manufacturing tenants typically pay less rent. One such area is New York's garment center.

Background

New York's garment center, located from Fifth Avenue to Tenth Avenue and from 34th to 41st Streets, has been the traditional home of the apparel industry in the United States since the turn of the century. The apparel industry is the city's largest manufacturing industry, employing more than 119,000 persons and producing $10 billion in goods annually. Coupled with 54,000 jobs in wholesale activities, the New York garment industry represents a $30 billion trade, accounting for more than 45 percent of the national total.[1] Not surprisingly, apparel industry groups such as the International Ladies Garment Workers Union wield considerable political clout in the City.

The Times Square Impact Study

In response to pressure from interests within the City's politically and economically influential apparel industry, Mayor Koch in 1984 directed the City's Planning Department to carry out a study of the potential impact of the nearby Times Square Redevelopment Project on the home of the American apparel industry, just one block south of the Redevelopment Project. Apparently, the impetus for this study was concern expressed about the future of the New York garment industry by the International Ladies Garment Workers Union. Some say that the Union had joined the City to support the Times Square project despite its fears that the strong Manhattan real estate market, particularly for office space, was placing substantial pressure on the garment industry and accelerating the loss of manufacturing jobs in the City. The Union's support of the Times Square project apparently was given on the condition that steps be taken to prevent additional damage to the industry by further accelerating the conversion of manufacturing space to other land uses, particularly offices. Arthur Margon, Executive Director of the Real Estate Board of New York City, told us:

> There had been rumors for several years that there was an agreement between the City and the Union, that the Union would not make a big fuss about 42nd Street, but it would get protective zoning of some sort....They can deliver a lot of votes and contributions. And more than that, they can deliver campaign workers. So it appears as if a deal was struck, and the result of the deal was the zoning in this area which protects manufacturing space from conversion to non-manufacturing uses. It was a totally unnecessary and uncalled-for sort of thing. And once the garment workers received this kind of zoning protection, we immediately began to hear other groups in the City demanding the same kind of protection—so that the furriers and hatters have asked for it and the theater people.

The study, which was undertaken by City staff and consultants, involved an unusually substantial commitment of City resources. The results showed indisputable evidence of an increasing rate of conversion of manufacturing/industrial space to office space as well as signs supporting each conversion such as the refusal to renew leases for manufacturing tenants or at least give long-term leases.[2] The study involved extensive surveys of existing conditions in the garment area and the market demands for various kinds of real estate in the city. The "culprit" the study blamed for the increasing rate of conversion was escalating rent pressure from potential office tenants willing to pay more than manufacturing/industrial tenants—a familiar land-use problem that has plagued maintenance of the status quo throughout the history of this country.

Simply stated, the study showed that office uses were displacing manufacturing/industrial uses. Unless something was done, the garment industry would be doomed as a significant city employer. The study's solution to the problem? A special district, of course (though Richard Satkin of the Department of City Planning describes this as a "reluctant

choice"). Ironically, the land-use pattern in the garment center that the City wanted to preserve—involving traffic congestion, trucks loading and unloading in the middle of the
street, overcrowded sidewalks, inadequate light and air, and
depressed land values and rents—is normally a condition
that zoning is employed to eliminate. Yet here these conditions, which most would describe as inferior, were about to
be the object of a preservation program because of the perceived threat to important City economic concerns.

Not everyone agreed that a special district was needed
or appropriate. Some felt that the garment industry was a
victim of market forces other than escalating rents and, thus,
could not be saved by preserving space alone. Joseph Rose of
Community Board No. 5 said:

> I haven't spoken to one person with any familiarity with
> real estate, with conversions of the nature of the district,
> office demand, demand for manufacturing space, [who]
> thinks that this can save one manufacturing job. The
> forces that determine whether manufacturing jobs sur-
> vive in the district have nothing whatsoever to do with
> office conversion.

Others concluded that traffic conditions were so bad
that the future of the garment industry was already at risk.
Raquel Ramati, a member of the original design group under
Mayor Lindsay, described for us the state of the garment district at that time:

> It's sort of funny that we always come into [a solution] so
> late, but then the garment district was such a mess be-
> tween the trucks, the curbcuts, the servicing. A rational
> plan would not make sense. We tried to do it for years
> without much success. And the truth is the garment in-
> dustry is in danger of being eliminated whether a special
> district could do anything for it or not.

The Special Garment Center District

The City refused, according to Norman Marcus, "to act
like King Canute shouting at the waves." It intended to re-

Special Garment Center District, looking west on 38th Street.
Photo: *J. B. White*

spond to the concerns of the garment industry, and it did. In 1987, the City created a special district in the twelve-block area from 35th Street to 40th Street and from Broadway to Ninth Avenue that limited the amount of manufacturing/industrial space that could be converted to office uses in specified areas. These provisions were described by some detractors as *"de facto* commercial rent control."

The Special Garment Center District attempts to preserve up to 8 million square feet (about 105 buildings) on the mid-blocks of the approximately 20 million square feet of manufacturing/industrial space occupied by the apparel industry. Owners are prohibited from converting this manufacturing space to office, business, professional, governmental, or veterinarian medicine use unless an amount of square

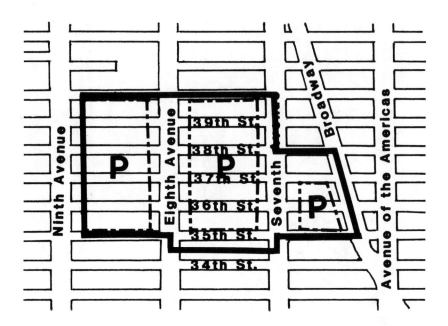

▬ Garment Center District

P Preservation Area

Special Garment Center District.
Source: *New York City Planning Commission*

footage equal to the space being converted is preserved for manufacturing. The space preserved can either be in the same building as the conversion (resulting in a mixed-use building) or in another building in the district's Preservation Area, which includes 40 percent of the total garment center apparel industry space. There is no limit on conversion of manufacturing/industrial space to showrooms, nor do the regulations apply to the frontages on the avenues in the district, including Broadway. Moreover, the district allows a wide range of manufacturing uses.

The Realtors Fight Back

Opponents of the new district, mostly property owners, argued that limiting the use of the buildings to manufacturing had the practical effect of controlling rents by eliminating market pressures on the district. In July, 1987, shortly after the district was adopted, a lawsuit was filed by the Real Estate Board of New York alleging that the adoption of the special district was unconstitutional because the owners of manufacturing/industrial space were denied all economic use of their property, and that the City had failed to comply with the State of New York's environmental impact statement requirements. The Board's position on the constitutional issue was largely based on written testimony submitted by a real estate expert, William Conway, who had carried out a study of real estate values in the garment center for the City but had ultimately opposed the adoption of the special district legislation.

At the time of the litigation, Conway disagreed with the City's view of the apparel industry and the garment district. According to Conway, office rents were not driving the manufacturers out; competition from overseas manufacturers was forcing New York manufacturers to cut costs by—among other things—seeking less expensive space. Landlords were left with no option but to solicit office tenants. In his affidavit, Conway wrote:

> If apparel manufacturers cannot afford higher rents, it is because their profit-margins are being eroded by global competitive pressures, not rent pressure....More important, apparel manufacturing and apparel manufacturing employment declined when rents were inexpensive, showing that the prime cause of decline is not rent. A zoning measure which removes the ability to create or lease to higher rent-paying uses is *de facto* commercial rent control, not zoning.[3]

The realtors pointed out that, in fact, the manufacturing components of the apparel industry had declined citywide by 40 percent during the previous fifteen years. The realtors apparently took no heart from the fact that, during that same time period, the wholesale and design components of the industry had increased by 25 percent. They believed that manufacturing would continue to decline, and landlords would be unable to rent their buildings. Empty space and abandoned buildings would have a far more severe impact on the neighborhood than would the conversion of manufacturing/industrial space to office space. The realtors also asserted, through their expert, that the office conversion opportunities contained in the special district were illusory because manufacturing/industrial uses and office uses are often, if not always, incompatible.

The other main element of the realtors' challenge was over the City's determination that it did not have to prepare an environmental impact statement for the proposed special district. The realtors' position was simple: manufacturing/industrial uses are much worse for the environment than office uses and, therefore, an environmental impact statement should have been prepared. Preparing the statement would have forced the City to evaluate reasonable alternatives to the special district. The realtors pointed out that offices need fewer, shorter truck deliveries than do manufacturing uses. This put the Koch administration in the ironic position of arguing that maintaining more crowded, congested traffic conditions, more noise, and more air pollution was in the best interests of the public health, safety, and welfare of the city—even though eliminating these conditions in the interest of the public health, safety, and welfare is zoning's traditional role. The City argued that no environmental impact statement was required because the special district did nothing more than maintain the status quo—the district regulations did not change a thing in the garment center.

In August, 1988, the trial court agreed with the realtors that the City should have prepared an environmental impact statement and ordered it to do so. Although it deferred a decision on the constitutional issue until after the impact statement was prepared, the trial court implied that if the realtors' economic assertions ultimately proved correct, "there might well be a constitutional problem."[4] The court reasoned that— unlike residential rent control situations where landlords are besieged by potential tenants—if garment district landlords are unable to find tenants who wish to lease their property for the uses permitted by the district and cannot convert the space to uses for which there is a market, the landlords may effectively be deprived of all use of their property.

The City appealed the court's order, and in May, 1990, the Appellate Division unanimously reversed the trial court, holding that the City "fully complied with applicable environmental laws." Of particular note is that the court found, even though it was not necessary for it to do so, that the scale of office conversions in the garment center posed "a serious threat to the economic future of New York City." The design of the district itself also received favorable comment from the court:

> The plan was so sensitive to other real estate needs that it restricted manufacturing uses of this center to only the mid-blocks, excluding the frontages on all the avenues, which could be developed into higher-renting showrooms or converted into offices.[5]

Presumably the petitioners will seek additional review by the highest court in New York State, but at least for now the Special Garment Center District is safe from facial attacks.

The District In Action

In the meantime, the City continues to study the garment area and to enforce the special district regulations. An unpublished 1990 door-to-door survey revealed that, contrary to the dire predictions of the realtors, vacancy rates have not increased within the district since its adoption. There have been few conversions since the regulations went into effect, although the recent "softness" of the general office market in New York is generally held responsible for this. Conversion activity just outside of the special district indicates some resistance to the regulations, but the ultimate success of the district is yet to be determined.

Success may also depend on the effectiveness of enforcement programs; illegal conversions are apparently quite easy and common, leaving no incentive to do authorized conversions. According to Sandy Hornick:

We all have doubts about whether or not you can really enforce the regulations; we think the economics work, but whether you can enforce the regulations in a situation where you aren't required to go to the Building Department when converting loft space to office space is another question. There's no hook that you can use to catch them.

Currently, however, the City has mounted a special enforcement effort in the district, designed to ensure that illegal conversions are detected and the ordinance enforced. Reportedly the City is ready to go to court on two major illegal office conversions. Perhaps this effort will deter others.

Conclusion

The Special Garment Center District is a good example of how a special district can provide a political solution for a common economic problem: protecting manufacturing uses in a city. It illustrates, as does the Clinton district, that special districts can be used to exclude the forces of affluence as well as the forces of decline. As long as it is reasonably enforced, the district will be successful in preserving the *space* it is intended to save—whether it is also successful in saving the *use* remains to be seen.

8

The Importance of Being Special

We all want to be special. We don't know that we're being specially foolish or specially duped or specially exploited.
Joanna Battaglia, Member,
Community Board No. 6

The professionals have serious doubts about special districts; the people, for the most part, believe they are great.

The City Planning staff and former professional employees believe that a good idea has been carried to ridiculous lengths; special districts are created for areas that have little special about them. Many in the Planning Commission believe that standard, generic zoning could be used to deal with local problems without the need to create a new special district for each neighborhood.

The residents, by contrast, get a psychological lift from residing in an area that has a tag to it—Little Italy or Clinton, for example. They know the special regulations; some of them know the twists and bends of the provisions of their districts as well as the lawyers do, and probably better than most of the administrators of the ordinance. They become, as Norman Marcus put it, "zoning freaks." Their zoning is the one part of the hopelessly complex myriad of municipal laws and policies that city residents believe they can understand. Don't ask residents how to solve the problems of the scary subways or garbage collection, or how to drive easily crosstown in Manhattan. But they can immediately spot a sign that violates the regulations of their special district or quickly detect a commercial establishment that operates in a way that is in violation of the labyrinthine district regulations.

Thus it appears that the professionals are losing a zoning conflict to the amateurs, a not unheard of event in the zoning arena. Two circumstances illustrate this conclusion. First, efforts by the planning staff to repeal two special districts have either failed in the face of neighborhood opposition, or, if successful, have taken years to accomplish. Second, in spite of staff skepticism about special districts, at least two additional districts have been added to the ordinance during the Koch administration, with a third under consideration now. We will consider the repeal attempts first.

Yorkville-East 86th Street

The Special Yorkville-East 86th Street District was one of the earliest mistakes. This section of East 86th Street between Park and First Avenues was once the shopping street for persons of German descent. It was a street with German bakeries, *haufbraus*, and *biergartens*, a miscellany of stores catering to Old World tastes. The zoning, however, was much more generous than the existing commercial uses required. In addition, there was a growing feeling among neighboring residents and Community Board No. 8 that the street was deteriorating with the introduction of fast-food shops and discount stores.

The catalyst for action was the construction in 1973 of a new, 400,000-square-foot Gimbels store at the corner of Lexington and 86th Streets. Residents felt that the way to prevent the intrusion of more big stores and fast-food chains was to limit the size of commercial establishments on the street. This led to the creation on May 29, 1974, of the Special Yorkville-East 86th Street District—commonly known as the "Anti-Gimbels District." This district imposed a maximum floor area of 100,000 square feet. More significantly, it set a maximum frontage of twenty-five feet for each establishment. A majority of the Commission believed that these and other provisions would halt the decline of the area

enough so that the locals could still enjoy a good wiener
schnitzel or a cool stein of beer in their favorite watering
place for some time to come.

Only one negative vote was cast at the Planning Commission meeting of April 3, 1974—by Commissioner Sylvia
Deutsch. Her objection is worth recording:

> In all the hearings and discussions about East 86th
> Street, I have tried to look at the Street as it has been pic-
> tured, but the words do not match my visual perception.
>
> East 86th Street is not unique. It had at one time a
> distinctive ethnic quality, and some of that is still there,
> but the Middle European charm and quality [are] fast
> disappearing. It's difficult now to distinguish between
> 86th Street and other active commercial areas of the
> City. It is, however, unique as a shopping area which
> does not reflect the type of luxury housing near it or the
> income levels of a number of the residents on the Upper
> East Side. It is, in short, an anomaly. This is 86th
> Street's problem.
>
> Community Planning Board No. 8 is one of the most
> conscientious and industrious in the city. They saw East
> 86th Street changing into a fast-food, short-order, quick
> turnover, discount street, and they began to look for a
> remedy which would stop the unwelcome change and
> bring back the charm. But the remedy we consider today
> will not do that.
>
> The proposed special district limits frontages to
> twenty-five feet on East 86th Street and fifty feet along
> the Avenue. This was ostensibly done to encourage the
> development of many specialty shops. But fast-food es-
> tablishments can still flourish and small specialty stores
> will not come in, regardless of frontage size, unless there
> is a market they can serve.[1]

Deutsch proved to be right. The fast-food joints proliferated.
What other type of store can get into twenty-five feet and
still pay the escalating rents?

Another former planner and a resident of the 86th
Street area has an alternative explanation for the neighbor-
hood's concern: "In my neighborhood, for example, when
Gimbels was built and the movie theater opened in the Gim-

Special Yorkville-East 86th Street District, now repealed.
Photo: *John Babcock*

bels, replacing the old RKO with a duplex instead of a simplex, the new facility attracted consumers from Harlem and the Bronx, and my wealthy neighbors objected to blacks coming into the neighborhood. And there began a real pressure to do something to keep further development of this sort from the neighborhood under the guise of trying to preserve the old ethnic character of the German neighborhood, which was by then disappearing."

Sandy Hornick, Director of the Zoning Study Group for the Planning Commission, calls Yorkville a "total failure." This sentiment is shared by many others. Martin Gallent, former Vice-Chairman of the Commission, acknowledged the mistake:

MG   [Yorkville] was an attempt to interfere with the process.
RFB With the market?
MG   Right. What Yorkville was, in effect, was an ethnic area. We in New York love ethnic areas. So we were seeing this ethnic area disintegrate. Here was a German, Slavic-type activity that was a benefit like Chinatown was a great benefit and Little Italy....We saw it slowly beginning to erode with high-rise developments and pricey stores and things like that. We said what can we do to preserve this? Here we are reaching beyond our camp. We didn't have enough knowledge about it. We said, maybe it is the size store. We won't allow stores that are more than twenty-five feet and, therefore, we'll keep the smaller store and that might work. Councilman Norman will never forget this: it was so outlandish—somebody said, why not make it only German stores? So we debated that and finally threw it out, but we were reaching, reaching to try to preserve what we saw as the best in the city, and that's what the special districts are. They don't always succeed. Yorkville did not succeed.

What the Commission had actually done was to accelerate the decline that had already set in. As rents escalated, only fast-food outlets could pay them, and more of the ethnic businesses moved out.

Despite many acknowledgements of failure, it still took fifteen years to correct the mistake. The Yorkville special district was finally removed from the books on June 29, 1989.

Special Park Improvement District

The Special Park Improvement District was another attempt that failed, or at least the most crucial element in it did. Nevertheless, an attempt by the Commission to repeal the district has been unsuccessful.

Central Park is the jewel of Manhattan. Designed more than a century ago by Frederick Law Olmsted, today it is somewhat tarnished in places and sullied by occasional muggings and headline-grabbing rapes and murders. The Park's main problem has been that the City did not have the financial means to maintain it properly.

Once again, the Planning Commission came up with what it thought was a good idea: why not have developers along Fifth Avenue and Park Avenue help pay for the upkeep of the Park? Thus, another special district was authorized on April 23, 1973: the Special Park Improvement District. The district runs along Fifth Avenue from 60th Street to 111th Street; it stretches up Park Avenue from 59th Street to 96th Street. The District lowered the FAR for buildings facing the Park, banned the bonus for plazas, and insisted on a uniform street line. If a builder wanted to get back the previously zoned FAR lost under this scheme, he would have to apply for a special permit and pay dollars into a fund for Park improvements.

According to those acquainted with the workings of this scheme, quite a bit of money went into the fund—perhaps a million dollars—but no one seems to know just what happened to the cash. A staff member said about the payments: "They got squandered somehow. And we didn't get any Park improvements. I don't really know what they did with it....It seemed like a good idea at the time, except that we've learned that taking money is a poor substitute for performance, in this city anyway. We didn't get anything for that money."

Norman Marcus told us:

> The money was put in a pot, and every Community Board with frontage on Central Park was on the committee to decide how the money should be spent. Can you picture that? Those meetings were described to me, and it was like a Tower of Babel because the communities were all so different. We had the Upper East Side community, very tony. We had the Midtown community, interested in business-type things. We had Board No. 7,

which is a West Side activist, socially conscious Board.
And then we had a couple of Harlem Boards with different agendas. They just didn't talk the same
language....The money sat for a long period of time and I
think the Park Department finally used it to clean up
graffiti. It did get spent after many years, but it was a
flawed idea from the outset.

Another staff member elaborated on the problem:

So the City has a chunk of money, doesn't necessarily
have a design, doesn't necessarily have the Parks Commissioner's decision on what was the highest priority.
Someone would argue we need the fountain on the west
side of the park, and someone would say, but a play-
ground that's two blocks from the new building is what's
really needed....The Commission may say the most important thing is the area nearest the East Side. And the
Parks Commissioner for perfectly good reason says near
the building is not where the Park needs improvement.
We need an improvement at 109th Street, which is
probably true. The Park is in worse condition at the
northern end.

By all accounts, the fund concept was a disaster. Not
only could no one agree on where the money should be
spent—some suspect the City comptroller simply put it in
the general fund—but the whole situation smacked of selling
zoning: you pay; you get your special permit. Eventually, on
April 4, 1982, the provision requiring a cash contribution
was removed from the district ordinance.

The staff, having an anti-special district bias, wanted to
go still farther and repeal the entire Special Park Improvement District. This effort to get rid of the district by the
Planning Commission failed. Basically, there was no constituency for a change, and there were still plenty of con-
stituencies for the district. North of 96th Street is the do-
main of Community Board No. 11 in East Harlem. The
Board had at least two objections to any change. First, the
proposed abolition of the district would involve a substantial
increase in the area's residential FAR, from 7.52 to 12. The
Board didn't want the increased bulk. Second, the Board

feared that gentrification would also result from the new developments. The popular perception—spread by a variety of organizations—was that the change would allow much larger buildings because the area would revert to the standard zoning for that part of Manhattan. Groups such as the Central Park Conservancy feared that larger buildings would somehow threaten the character of Central Park. Thus, for different reasons, different areas strongly opposed removal of the special district. That opposition remains today, and so does the district.

The message of the Special Park Improvement District seems clear: if a city is intrigued by the special district concept, beware; if it turns out to be pointless or even counterproductive, repeal may be difficult. People simply do not want to give up the label.

Union Square

These special neighborhood zoning ordinances are so attractive that the skepticism of the central planning staff has been overcome in the creation of at least two new districts during the Koch administration.

The Special Union Square District illustrates how special districts can be misused to cover up spot zoning. Union Square lies at the intersection of 14th Street and Fifth Avenue. It comprises about three city blocks, extending up to 17th Street. Fifth Avenue continues past it on the east and Broadway is its western boundary. Decades ago, the Square was the hub of the city. As fancy stores and expensive housing moved north up Fifth Avenue, the Square deteriorated until it became a hangout for drug pushers and prostitutes. Sex shops and other sleazy establishments sprouted up around it. Vacant storefronts proliferated. Klein's, a block-long discount store on the West Side, closed down ten or fifteen years ago, and this abandoned building became an eyesore. Practically the only evidence left of the Square's former heyday were the multiple subway lines that merged there. From Union Square one can travel almost anywhere in the City by subway.

In 1985, Zeckendorf & Company became interested in acquiring the Klein site to erect four towers, each twenty-seven stories high. The first four stories would be commercial; the balance would consist of market-rate condos. In order to build these towers, the developer needed more FAR than was allowed by the generic zoning for that area. The City, which had been trying to clean up the Square, wanted Zeckendorf to proceed. How to accommodate him? If the City simply upzoned the Klein site alone, there was always the risk that some person or group would allege an illegal spot zoning. As one planner explained:

> Sometimes City Planning uses a special district as spot zoning, to get around the charge of spot zoning. So they create a special district which has really one objective, which is to upzone a certain site. Union Square is a classic example of that and [the staff will] acknowledge it. They'll say, look, we had to get around the charge of just doing spot zoning, so we created this district.

The district, adopted on January 10, 1985, changed the FAR around Union Square in different amounts. The north and west sides received a modest increase, while the south and part of the eastern area were given very big increases. In general, residential uses received larger FAR increases than commercial. Commercial FAR was capped at 6; residential FAR varied: in some places it was raised to 8, the Klein site to 10. A bonus of 2 FAR was offered for subway connections. A street mall was mandated as well as ground floor retail.

We asked Conn Howe, now head of City Planning staff, why Union Square was any different than a dozen other squares in New York City. He replied:

> I think the tendency will be not even to have to do it, call that a special district. What we would do instead is have a generic zone that had a streetwall requirement and just use that. In fact, we're looking at the rest of 14th Street and we are specifically not looking at a special district designation. We're looking at one of our "contextural zones," which requires a streetwall and sky exposure plan and, actually, some of our generic and some of our contextural zones also require the retail continuity.

Zeckendorf building at the southeast corner of Union Square.
Photo: *J. B. White*

So we get everything except the differential between commercial and residential. We can even control that because some of our contextural zones have a limit, could be 2 FAR of commercial.

Another staff member was more candid: "In my opinion, in this instance, it was used as a way of avoiding focusing attention off the [Zeckendorf] project and on to the [special] district." Sneaky.

Grand Concourse

It should not be surprising that most of New York's special districts are in Manhattan. It is the oldest area of the city, and it abounds with land-use anomalies such as Clinton.

There is, however, one boulevard in the West Bronx that may truly be called special: the Grand Concourse. It is one of the few streets that resisted—and survived—the deterioration of the South Bronx in the 1960s and 1970s. In the case of the Grand Concourse, we can see another twist of the special district dynamic: neighborhood branch offices of City Planning are often quite enthusiastic about special districts regardless of what the central staff thinks.

The idea of a grand boulevard for the Bronx was conceived in the 1890s. Louis Risse, an engineer inspired by the work Baron Georges Houssman did in Paris for Louis Napoleon in the 1850s, imagined a roadway connecting Manhattan with park lands in North and Central Bronx that would rival the Champs Elysees. A report by the Bronx Office of the City Planning Department in 1986 describes Risse's creation:

> The four and one-half mile road was 182 feet wide and ran from 161st Street to Mosholu Parkway. An unusually wide road, the Grand Concourse had tree-lined malls and featured an express dirt-and-cinder speedway for horse-drawn carriages and paved service lanes that accommodated local traffic. In addition, a system of underpasses was built at major intersections to permit east-west traffic to pass under the Grand Concourse

ridge without interfering with the speedway above, making the Grand Concourse one of the nation's first grade-separated highways.[2]

Originally the Concourse, dedicated in 1909, ran from 161st Street north to Mosholu Parkway, but it was extended south to 138th Street in the 1920s. There were no trolley lines; this was a street for carriages and promenading. The most well-known building was the Concourse Plaza Hotel on East 161st Street. It was the center of social, sporting, and political life in the area, widely publicized as the place where the great Yankee teams of the 1920s stayed. The hotel hung on into the late 1920s, when it finally succumbed. Today it is housing for the elderly under the Section 8 program.

A great deal of housing was constructed along the Concourse in the 1920s. In the 1930s, another building boom took place. According to the same report, "approximately forty Art Deco-style apartment buildings and a new Art Deco county courthouse [were] built. This activity gave the West Bronx the largest collection of Art Deco buildings in the United States."[3] The buildings along the Concourse have a remarkable uniformity of scale. Facade continuity was achieved not by public regulation but by the small number of architects, who often developed whole blocks at one time.

The post-World War II decay that cursed other parts of the Bronx did not hit the Concourse as severely. Some people did move out to the suburbs and to Co-op City, but, in general the population decline has been lower than the average decline citywide. What has happened is the conversion of ground-floor residential units into commercial and office establishments, threatening the residential character of the Concourse.

Perhaps the most noticeable intrusions are the small bodegas that reflect the changing demographic pattern of the street; many of them are illegal conversions or conversions done with variances where the owner or renter did not comply with the condition of the variance. Gaudy signs and canopies often hide the original design of the street. Actually, most conversions have not been to stores but to offices, primarily small law offices taking advantage of the proximity of the Bronx County Courthouse.

Special Grand Concourse District, looking north.
Photo: *John Babcock*

A 1985 survey by the Planning Commission staff located 216 commercial uses along the residential portions of the Grand Concourse. More than half of these (125) were illegal. Another ninety were nonconforming uses made legal by variances subject to many conditions. The restrictions written into these variances were very strict. Bakeries, delicatessens, and stores that sold meat or fish were usually prohibited; signs could only be painted on store windows. Because most of these conditions in the variances were ignored by the tenants, many of the nonconforming uses were still illegal despite the variances they had.

In 1985, the Bronx office of the Planning Department began preparation of a Special Grand Concourse District. As the 1986 report explained:

> In order to fulfill the City's objectives to preserve the residential quality of the Grand Concourse and to direct and encourage desirable changes, City Planning recommends the establishment of a special zoning district for the Concourse. This solution, as opposed to conventional zoning

changes, would allow legalization of certain types of uses where they are considered appropriate, but would not open up the Concourse for unchecked commercial uses.[4]

The proposed Special Grand Concourse District would create a Residential Preservation Area, a Limited Commercial Area, and Commercial Overlay Extensions. The district would impose severe design controls in residential areas, for example: "The color of replacement windows installed after April, 1986, would be limited to a shade of black or brown," and "Residential canopies would have to be made of canvas or other heavy fabric; rigid plastic or metal canopies would not be permitted."[5] The Limited Commercial Area would make more than fifty illegal stores legal. Here, too, design controls would be very strict, including prescriptions for sign colors and size of window graphics.

The Commercial Extension Area included some cross-streets where commercial uses—again often illegal—had been creeping up to the Concourse. Under the district's terms, commercial development would be allowed to extend to the Grand Concourse "on the basement floor only provided that no signs, advertisements, or display windows were located within fifty feet of the Concourse."[6] Probably twenty-five illegal businesses would be legalized by these terms.

The Planning Commission approved the proposal and went through the long process of public review by the various Community Boards through whose areas the Concourse runs. The Special Grand Concourse District was finally approved by the Board of Estimate on September 28, 1989. It is too early to tell if it has been successful.

Special Grand Central Station Subdistrict

Now, yet another special subdistrict is proposed by the Planning Commission. The area around Grand Central Terminal has been controlled by the regulations of the Special Midtown District. The Terminal, of course, is an historic landmark. As such, it can transfer all of its approximately 1.7 mil-

lion square feet of unused development rights to sites immediately adjacent or in a chain of ownership. This provision
was used in 1979 to grant a special permit to allow the con-
veyance of 74,655 square feet of development rights from the
Terminal to the southwest corner of 42nd Street and Park Avenue to facilitate the construction of the Philip Morris headquarters. This resulted in an office building with a 21.6 FAR.

The problem, as the Planning Commission saw it, was
the impossibility of controlling the distribution of the large
amount of development rights available to the Terminal.
These rights could, under Midtown regulations, be distributed over an area defined primarily by the Terminal's
complicated ownership patterns rather than by appropriate
planning concerns. In particular, there was no limit on the
amount of development rights which could be transferred to
any one site; this was left to the discretion of the Planning
Commission and the Board of Estimate.

The Planning Commission's November, 1989, report to
the Board of Estimate concluded that: "Collectively, these circumstances make it clear that the current regulations could
lead to an ad hoc series of applications for the transfer of development rights."[7]

A new special subdistrict would, according to the report:

1. Permit the excess development rights from Grand Central Terminal to be distributed over a wider area defined by the extensive pedestrian circulation network;
2. Place a cap on the total amount of development rights
   which may be transferred to any individual site;
3. Establish a mechanism for making and evaluating
   pedestrian circulation improvements; and
4. Specify bulk regulations to enhance the subdistrict's
   special character.[8]

The boundaries of the subdistrict would extend from
East 41st to 48th Streets, from the midblock west of Madison
Avenue to the midblock east of Lexington Avenue. There
would be a "core" area between the center lines of Madison
and Lexington Avenues.

All sites within the subdistrict would be eligible, by authorization of the Planning Commission, to receive up to 1

FAR of development rights from landmarked buildings. The urban plaza bonus would be eliminated. Sites within the "core" area would be eligible for a transfer of development rights up to a maximum of 21.6 FAR by special permit from the Planning Commission. In addition, numerous urban design controls would be mandated.

In spite of the growling of the staff that there are already too many special districts, one more is moving to approval.

Conclusion

The events described in this chapter illustrate the capacity of special districts to survive attempts at eradication and to appear—like a rash—in yet another area of the zoning epidermis. Indisputably, their survival could not have occurred without the blessings of the people.

Special districts may do no more than tell residents that they are recognized by City Hall, elevated, if you will, to a unique status in this gigantic, impersonal—if not inhuman—metropolis. Even when created for questionable purposes or to get one or another pressure group off the backs of the bureaucrats, special districts are still appearing, and we can expect that more will follow.

9

San Francisco

The Commercial Street
Where You Live

Once you give a district its own name, the community that is involved in that district takes hold of it and will not let it go.

Robin Jones, City Planner

Most of my clientele won't propose anything in the special districts—they are too political.

San Francisco Architect

New York City is not the only place where special districts have been used. San Francisco's experience can give us another perspective on the elements that are typical of special districts everywhere.

Although San Francisco began using special districts in earnest somewhat later than New York, they originated out of the same coalescence of innovative city planners and dedicated neighborhood associations as created the phenomenon in New York. Now, San Francisco has more special districts than New York in proportion to its population—a total of sixteen.

An interesting difference between the two cities is that most of San Francisco's special districts are all the same type: neighborhood commercial districts. The regulation of relatively small commercial corridors in residential areas seems to have been the one zoning problem that the City did not choose to solve or could not solve through its general zoning ordinance.

Background

Unlike New York, where special districts arose in the wake of problems created by a revised zoning ordinance, the special district story started in San Francisco as part of the mid-1970s comprehensive revision to the city's ordinance. With the exception of overlay zones for garment shops and signs, the city, up to that point, had survived with only generic districts.

During the analysis of existing regulations and the inventory of the commercial areas that was part of the revision process, city planners identified a new need. They realized that there were discrete neighborhood commercial areas that had particular characteristics and needs that did not fit into the four generic neighborhood commercial districts that existed in the general ordinance. These commercial areas were typified by small-scale, neighborhood-based retail combined with second- and third-story residential units. They were located in the midst of large, fairly cohesive neighborhoods, often along major thoroughfares.

Catalyst: Union Street

San Francisco's first experiment with special districts occurred on Union Street. This district became the prototype for all of the city's other special neighborhood commercial districts. Union Street is a primarily commercial corridor characterized by many upper-story dwelling units and offices and almost completely surrounded by residentially zoned lots. Until the 1970s, it had been a very sleepy, quiet neighborhood commercial strip with lots of the kinds of businesses—drugstores, shoe stores, and others—that mainly served the convenience of the surrounding neighborhood.

In the early 1970s, fashionable boutiques began to open on the street, attracting patronage from throughout the city. Terry Pimsleur, a neighborhood activist, recalls that the street began this "renaissance" in the 1960s and rapidly became a "trendy" tourist street. The neighborhood groups became concerned that the street's typical Victorian buildings were being replaced with "insurance modern." More seriously, restaurants were displacing the smaller retail merchants; the number of restaurants and bars in the ten-block area had grown from ten in 1947 to forty-seven in 1978. The neighborhood-oriented businesses were being driven out and entertainment uses were proliferating, bringing with them congestion, parking problems, and early morning noise. The residents became determined to halt this trend.

The first thing the neighborhood tried was to protect itself through historic designation. This attempt failed because the area did could not qualify under the historic district standards. Next, a group of residents—property owners, merchants, and business people—took their problem to the District Supervisor, Dianne Feinstein. She promised to direct the attention of the Planning Department to the needs of the area.

The Union Street Neighborhood Commercial District

The Planning Department got to work. While the district was being studied, the city planners imposed a one-year moratorium on the approval of bars, restaurants, and branch banks. Later, in 1979, they adopted interim controls, which were known as the Union Street Special Use District. The neighborhood land-use inventory prepared at the supervisor's request revealed that there was one bar for every 250 feet and one restaurant for every 100 feet of commercial frontage on Union Street. Since the community was definitely upset over this amount, the planners made the logical assumption that this density represented "enough" for the area. The interim controls provided that the existing density of bars and restaurants would be the threshold and that above that number, a conditional use would be required.

The early drafts of the permanent regulations limited certain types of uses in the district and prescribed the specific number of bars, restaurants, and banks that would be allowed. Later, in the neighborhood commercial rezoning

San Francisco

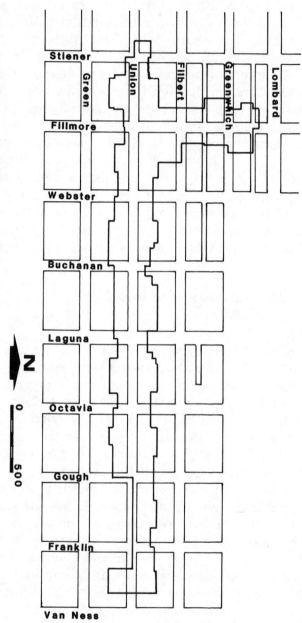

Union Neighborhood Commercial District, San Francisco.
Source: San Francisco Department of City Planning

study, those absolute numbers were translated into proportional limitations based on the lineal footage of the street currently devoted to that use. If the threshold was exceeded, a conditional use was still possible in most instances. Some uses in the permanent district controls were prohibited entirely. In some of the later special districts—Haight and Clement, for example—the early Union Street example was made even stricter; no new restaurants, bars, take-out food, or fast-food uses were permitted at all.

A Planning Commissioner who also owns a small business told us that the neighborhood commercial regulations first used on Union Street reflect a total lack of understanding of retailing. Particularly offensive to him were the regulations that prohibited a successful retailer from expanding without having to move out of the district. According to the Commissioner, a successful retailer sets higher standards for surrounding uses and draws additional consumers into the area, yet he was able to cite several instances where the maximum square footage provisions of special districts such as Union Street forced these entrepreneurs to either abandon their plans or move elsewhere.

Other nonconforming uses in the neighborhood commercial districts are treated more kindly than in other kinds of zoning districts. Although the district regulations say that no more restaurants, banks, and the like may enter the neighborhood commercial districts, those that are already there are welcome and may expand or increase the intensity of their use. In addition, if a particular restaurant in a neighborhood commercial district, for example, goes out of business, and no other permitted use (such as a shoe store) wishes to move into that site, then another restaurant can be established at that location. Moreover, if a restaurant wants to move within a district, and if a deed restriction is placed against the title of the original location of the restaurant so that the site can never be used for a restaurant again, then the restaurant may relocate anywhere in the district. Nonconforming restauranteurs also are able to move to a locale where another restaurant is currently located. The goal of these regulations is to allow existing prohibited uses some flexibility while ensuring that the net amount of prohibited uses does not increase.

Has Union Street worked? The verdict is still out. Some describe the area as an immensely successful regional shopping street. Others point out with considerable satisfaction that the district is such a "success" that fast-food franchises do not even try to locate there. The District was even able to force Seven-Eleven to do an 1880s-style store, the only one in the United States at one point that was not open twenty-four hours. On the flip side, critics of the district say that rents have become so high that many of the small stores that were originally targeted for protection have been forced out anyway.*

San Francisco's Neighborhood Commercial Special Districts

The neighborhood commercial district prototype developed on Union Street turned out to be applicable—with modifications—to many parts of the city. Robin Jones and Inge Horton of the San Francisco Department of City Planning, two of the chief architects of the city's special district concept, told us that by the time they got through the Union Street study, nine additional streets had come to the Planning Department claiming that they needed similar types of controls. Special districts became the "thing to do" to protect the neighborhood. Jones recounted:

> Pretty soon we were covering the entire city....Pretty soon we were up to our knees in a whole range of issues and a whole set of controls.

While developing the neighborhood commercial special districts, the Planning Department worked with 10,000 parcels in over 200 locations throughout the city (excluding the down-

*Since the initial interviews for this chapter, the Seven-Eleven store was closed and there are many vacant stores. Two major competing shopping centers and a general over-abundance of retail are reported to be among the causative factors, in addition to the slowness of tourism since the earthquake.

town, south of Market, the Fisherman Wharf area and China-town). All of these districts had two common themes: preserving upper-floor residential units in commercial buildings, and keeping fast-food restaurants from taking over the street.

What emerged was a comprehensive revision of the zoning ordinance as it related to neighborhood-oriented commercial areas (see Appendix D). A new article of the Planning Code was developed to establish four new generic districts and sixteen special district classifications, tailor-made variations to the generic districts. The Planning Code regulations were complemented by extensive use and design guidelines in the City's Master Plan.

The conversion of second-floor residential units to offices was a hot issue, especially in areas such as North Beach. This second- and occasionally third-floor housing was considered a reservoir of affordable housing and residential hotels. Its disappearance eroded the heterogeneity of a neighborhood and was believed to contribute to its gentrification.

Another thorn in the side of neighborhood residents was restaurants, particularly fast-food establishments. No one likes food wrappers in his or her neighborhood; no one likes the traffic and parking problems generated by full-service restaurants; no one likes the destruction of architecturally significant buildings to conform to the corporate style of a restaurant chain. On the other hand, the vocal and politically strong immigrant community views restaurant food service as an important entry to employment and economic independence for new arrivals to this country. Thus, some compromises were negotiated: a fast-food restaurant in a neighborhood commercial district was permitted to occupy an old building at a prominent location on the condition that it restore the facade and conform to signage controls.

North Beach

A particularly interesting area to which the special district idea spread is North Beach. Traditionally, North Beach had been an Italian area. Robin Jones described the area in the early 1980s:

[It was] a neighborhood transitioning to Chinese, a lot of Yuppies, intense, exciting part of town, walking distance to Chinatown, to downtown, to the waterfront, very high real estate values, property values, and a host of changes going on, old-time coffeehouses, old-time pasta factories, coffee-roasting plants that have been there for half a century being replaced by franchised fast-food, Asian restaurants, branch banks, upper-story dwelling units being converted to architects' offices. Everything that's happening in the city in different parts and different pieces is all happening in North Beach.

Jane Winslow, President of the Telegraph Hill Dwellers, a large and powerful neighborhood association, characterized the "charm" of North Beach as low-scale "hodgepodgey"—delis, butcher shops, and narrow storefronts.

The area was under pressure because of its close proximity to the downtown financial district and waterfront. Enterprising owners and developers wanted to put in cheap office space on the second and third floors and convert the low-cost housing into touristy kinds of hotels and bed-and-breakfast accommodations.

The neighbors wanted the special character of the area protected from this trend but not regulated quite so strongly as Union Street; they believed too much design control would produce just another "cutesy" area. The result was a district where many uses became highly regulated, such as financial institutions and fast-food restaurants, but the regulations themselves do not emphasize Victorian vernacular architecture.

Comparison with New York City

San Francisco has faced most of the same issues that New York City has in its special districts. Administrative problems are particularly common in both cities.

As in New York, everyone acknowledges that the special district regulations are complex. The Assistant Planning Director, George Williams, referred to them as "a nightmare to administer." A Planning Commissioner described his role as

a "referee of space." Clearly, the regulations originally designed to protect the "little guy" have become maneuverable
only by the very sophisticated or the very powerful.

On the other hand, no one has suggested an alternative.
The Planning Department attempted to help users cope with
the complexity by printing a table that summarized all of the
controls for every district. It is true that, given a reasonable
amount of explanation or prior experience with such matters,
the table is helpful. But it is not helpful enough, and a new
breed of urban professional, the "permitting expediters,"
have taken their place in the economic structure of the city.

A number of senior planning staff professionals consider
the need for coordination between the different departments
in charge of administering these districts to be a serious implementation problem. "The sheer weight and massiveness of
the effort generates caseload work that our staff is just crum-
bling under."

A particularly vocal critic of the Planning Department
cited the City's failure to establish a monitoring program to
determine the districts' economic effects on retailing as a
particularly troublesome issue, though it does not seem
likely that current staffing could accomplish very much in
this area. And yet there are still some who say that there are
not enough regulations.

The Role of the Citizen

As in New York, giving a zoning district the name of an
established neighborhood ensures that the district is here to
stay. The communities in Castro, North Beach, Sacramento
Street, and Clement will never let their districts go, even
though the controls are not that different from district to district. Even though it might be more efficient to consolidate
all of the special districts into one category of the standard
zoning code, politically the City "can't go back," predict Robin
Jones and Inge Horton.

The City has been able to resist the temptation to add a
special district to handle every known problem area. Tech-

niques to avoid adding special districts include inserting "subdistricts" into some of the generic zoning districts where additional regulations only apply to the smaller area, and limiting particular uses, such as fast-food restaurants, only in areas where the limits are really needed.

San Francisco, too, has been vastly assisted by the "professional citizen" who acts as adjunct staff, counting bars and restaurants, "tattling" and calling in complaints. In a classic understatement, Assistant Planning Director George Williams described San Francisco as a "vigilant community." Some people express fears that this vigilance might enable the misuse of district standards to keep out certain ethnic or economic groups. But given the economic strains on the city as a result of the 1989 earthquake, this dependence on the citizenry for enforcement is likely to continue.

San Francisco did try to alleviate its enforcement problem by adopting an "amnesty period" of three years for illegal conversions. During this period, an applicant could "legalize" an illegal conversion upon application and review. Latest reports indicate that this has not worked; very few applications have even been received.

One New York institution that has not developed in San Francisco is the formalization of the neighborhood association into a Community Board or its equivalent. There was considerable citywide interest expressed in this concept, whereby a board appointed by the Board of Supervisors would review and comment on all applications for development approval within its jurisdiction. But the political structure did not adopt the idea. The neighborhood groups effectively exercise this control anyway, ensuring that few, if any, proposals they oppose are approved.

Conclusion

It is clear from the San Francisco experience that special districts can be quite successful outside the New York City context. Moreover, San Francisco's experience shows that they may be appropriate for achieving a number of diverse planning goals: limiting the numbers of particular uses; limiting the expansion of some uses; protecting housing; and protecting the character of the neighborhood. It is also gratifying to note that even in a city with highly sophisticated planners and a frequently agitated group of citizens, a good idea does not necessarily have to run amok. Barnett's "penicillin effect" did not occur in San Francisco.

Chicago

Industrial-Strength Zoning

A phenomenal success.
Alderman Edwin Eisendrath,
Chicago Tribune Magazine, February 2, 1990

PMDs are a rather modest zoning innovation. They reinforce current manufacturing zoning and signal the development community that the city will not approve incremental conversions. With PMDs in place, speculative pressures should diminish, creating the opportunity for new industrial development.
R. Giloth and J. Betancur, Summer, 1988,
reprinted by permission of the *Journal of
the American Planning Association*

It makes it very difficult to sell my property.
David Schopp, Chairman, U.S. Sample Co.,
Chicago Tribune Magazine, February 2, 1990

One manifestation of the special district concept is the generic special district. This is created when enabling language in the zoning ordinance allows a certain kind of special district to be applied to more than one location in the city. The city of Chicago has developed a generic special district to protect manufacturing uses. The "Planned Manufacturing District" (PMD), Chicago's version of New York's Garment Center district, was adopted by the City Council in 1988. It is the "baby" of community activists, nurtured by the enlightened support of Independent Alderman Martin Oberman and his successor, Edwin Eisendrath. As we shall see, the district is an unusual achievement in the face of Chicago's traditional emphasis on zoning by politics.

Background

Chicago developed the Planned Manufacturing District in response to a citywide loss of industrial and manufacturing jobs in the 1970s and 1980s. Between 1978 and 1987, the city of Chicago experienced a downtown building boom that totalled about $7.2 billion.[1] During this same period, the city lost between 100,000 and 144,000 manufacturing jobs (the number varies by source).[2] Some sources put the city's loss of industrial space between the years 1982 and 1988 at 5,856,954 square feet or 35.5 percent.[3] The area known as the "SuperLoop," eleven square miles that include the traditional downtown, gained 76,400 mostly service-related jobs during the same period. The part of this area known as the South Loop, formerly a center for printing and publishing, by 1988 had over 6,000 middle- to high-income residents—having displaced forty-five largely industrial and manufacturing firms.[4] Once the dominant employer, manufacturing by 1986 had slipped to second place in Chicago, behind the service sector.[5]

City policies reinforced this displacement of manufacturing. According to one source, the City granted many Industrial Revenue Bonds in the SuperLoop for largely nonmanufacturing projects, including the renovation of Dearborn Station in the South Loop.[6] City zoning policies also strengthened the loss of the city's manufacturing and industrial base. From 1984 to 1988, there were 139 rezonings from manufacturing to residential or residential support uses (such as retail), with little opportunity for manufacturers to voice opposition.[7] Part of the problem was that, in Chicago, many zoning decisions are decentralized, left in the hands of neighborhood politicians. Ironically, this strong local power also facilitated the adoption of the PMD. Former Independent Alderman Martin Oberman described the situation:

> We needed a better industrial policy than just one that
> Alderman Oberman happened to make up on the spur of

the moment at a community meeting. There isn't any city policy. There isn't anything in the zoning code that said I could or could not do this [adopt a special district]. I just did it.[8]

Pressure on the Near North River Corridor

Concern over the loss of manufacturing in the city first became focused on an area just north of downtown Chicago known as the Near North River Corridor, where an important part of the city's industrial and manufacturing life has made its home since the turn of the century. According to the Chicago Association of Neighborhood Development Organizations (CANDO) in 1988, "roughly 350 firms providing 20,000 industrial jobs exist in the Corridor, or about 8 percent of Chicago's manufacturing base. About 70 percent of the employees of these companies are Chicago residents, a remarkably large percentage of whom live in the neighborhood."[9]

Like other parts of the city, the Near North River Corridor area was witnessing the loss of industrial/manufacturing land to residential and commercial uses. A stimulant for the concept of a new special district came in the early 1980s when a developer purchased an industrial building in a part of the Near North River Corridor area he acerbically described as having a "museumlike quality...[with vestiges of] manufacturing techniques from another century."[10] While others had a different assessment of the vibrancy of the area, no one in Chicago would have presumed to stop his conversion of a former piano factory to residential lofts. According to the *Chicago Tribune*:

> A collective shudder...rippled through the industrial landowners. Since then [1984] the relentless force of affluent Lincoln Park [to the east] has spilled over into North Avenue and pushed west right up to Clybourn Avenue, where, for the moment, it has stopped.[11]

The vacancy rate of industrial land was almost zero, demand was high, and yet ever more rezonings were occurring.

Near North River Corridor, Chicago.
Source: *Chicago Tribune*

Chicago was losing industry, not just because of taxes or labor costs but because there was insufficient land to expand.
Any vacant land that did become available was being
snapped up by retail and housing developers. By 1987, the
pressure for retail development was intense (even more than
for office space in New York) along Clybourn Avenue, the
main artery for the Near North River Corridor. At first, the
manufacturing concerns did not oppose new retail development because it was considered a good "buffer" between industrial and residential uses. Eventually, the manufacturers

began to realize that retail uses posed similar threats as residential development—higher property values and taxes, increased traffic, competition for parking, and conflicts over noise and other characteristics of manufacturing operations.

The City began to realize that stability had to be provided to the rezoning process so that manufacturers would feel secure enough to further invest in the city through expansion of their facilities. A Planned Manufacturing District began to look like a good solution.

Industrial uses faced another threat besides simple lack of space. The new residents who were moving in to areas such as the Near North River Corridor complained about living next door to industrial and manufacturing uses (the classic "latest on the block" syndrome). Ironically, state laws require that manufacturing uses must not inconvenience neighboring residents with noise, bad odors, or any of the other conditions commonly associated with industry even if the residents move in to an area adjacent to an already existing manufacturing use. Residential conversions were thus accelerating the loss of manufacturing space by forcing remaining companies to comply to stricter codes or move.

The Coalition

According to Gregory Longhini, former Director of Industrial Planning for the City, the PMD could never have been engineered without the support of a coalition of strange bedfellows—community organizations, industry, residents, and aldermen—that carried an initially reluctant Planning Department along.

In the Near North River Corridor, community leaders, including Donna Ducharme of the Local Employment and Economic Development Council (LEED Council), "don't get any better", according to Longhini. Their knowledge and their ability to build the requisite coalition made the City's job to create a district a lot easier.

The PMD also received important support from the major industrial and manufacturing concerns in the area. Characterized by the *Tribune* as the "strongest proponent of the Clybourn PMD,"[12] A. Finkl & Sons, a steel-forging manufacturer with 430 employees in the Clybourn area, was clearly a major player in the coalition. Finkl was typical of the larger companies whose ability to remain in the area was critical to their continued vitality. In contrast, the smaller companies, which had smaller investments in the area, were less supportive of the proposed district. Not having a major investment in land and plant tying them to the location, these smaller companies placed more importance on the appreciation in the value of their real estate created by the rezonings than on remaining in the area. In Longhini's view, the single most significant factor in the success of the district was the presence of major businesses, such as Finkl, who were willing to put their money and their influence behind adoption of the district. Many of these businesses participated financially in what, at many points, amounted to a public relations campaign.

In addition, the PMD received support from area residents. These supporters may not have been as interested in saving the businesses themselves as they were in achieving related objectives: increasing parking requirements and prohibiting fast-food restaurants.

The final member of the coalition was the City itself: the mayor and the aldermen. The coalition found a very receptive administration in City Hall, as Mayor Harold Washington had campaigned on a platform based in large part on the need to save manufacturing and industrial jobs for the city. This support was coupled with the critical backing of the affected aldermen.

Even the smallest child knows that the aldermen really control zoning in Chicago. According to Martin Oberman:

> There is a venerable unwritten Chicago institution that the local alderman is king or queen in his own ward, which I think is very essential to all zoning situations, good and bad. I am told this is relatively unique to Chicago. In few other major cities do you have to go to some local politician who has a life or death say over your land use.[13]

Thus, Aldermen Martin Oberman and Edwin Eisendrath were able to get the Planned Manufacturing District adopted in spite of the opposition of a number of influential developers.

The Planned Manufacturing District

The special district the City devised was an "enabling" district—some would call it a "floating zone"—that allowed the application of the district to particular parts of the city. The district was not intended to be automatically applied to any area, even though there were obvious candidates for its use. Either the mayor, all owners of land within the boundaries of the proposed district, or the alderman of the area can propose a district. Upon application, there is a review and hearing process, during which the applicant must present the Planning Commission with evidence regarding certain identified factors, largely directed at the continued viability of the area for industrial and manufacturing uses.

The district provides that no residential uses will be permitted in the area to which it is applied and that "supplementary regulations" specifying prohibited uses and other restrictions will be developed and adopted by City Council for each area when the district is actually applied to the zoning map. In essence, the Planned Manufacturing District merely set forth very general parameters for its application, leaving the details to be worked out for each particular location.

Clybourn Corridor

The first area where the new district was actually applied was the Clybourn Corridor, the "heart" of the Near North River Corridor. The Clybourn Corridor is an area of 115 acres containing thirty-one industrial firms from seventeen different industrial groups and about 1,700 employees. In 1988, R. Giloth and J. Betancur noted in the *Journal of the American Planning Association*:

> If speculative redevelopment continues [in the Clybourn area], most firms in the district are likely to relocate because of high rents and property taxes, evictions, lack of adequate space to expand, hard-to-refuse purchase offers, and conflict with new land uses.[14]

The fate of one defunct foundry before the PMD was implemented is a good example of the kinds of pressures that were instrumental in the development of the PMD for the Clybourn area. After this foundry had gone out of business, the property was purchased for a large shopping center. Unfortunately, the property was located adjacent to A. Finkl & Sons, and the siting of a shopping center there would have made the steel company in violation of Illinois anti-noise laws. A compromise was reached, resulting in Finkl's purchase of a portion of the foundry property and the development of a scaled-down shopping center on the remaining land. The developer of the shopping center agreed to ensure that substantial efforts would be made to employ residents of the area (presumably displaced by the loss of industrial and manufacturing jobs).

The developer also agreed to purchase an industrial site close to the shopping center site, "advancing the cost for acquisition, site development, market studies, plans, both architectural and engineering and the *pro formas* required for financing."[15] The site would be designed for small industrial users, ranging in area between 1,500 square feet to 10,000 square feet; the developer's obligation to provide the site was not linked to obtaining actual users. There were additional provisions in the agreement regarding the nature of the improvements (in part to ensure that a mini-warehouse was not constructed) and the tenants' leases, which had to contain a prohibition on using more than 30 percent of the space for office purposes. The developer was required to obtain the site immediately and commence development within two years. A "back out" clause was provided whereby, if the developer could not proceed with the contemplated development due to "market changes outside of its control,"[16] he would grant the City a two-year option to purchase the site for industrial development at the original acquisition price.

Train traveling along Lakewood Avenue, Clybourn district, Chicago.
Photo: © *Copyrighted, Chicago Tribune Company, all rights reserved, used with permission.*

The developer will have no trouble disposing of his site. Reportedly, there has been significant interest by industrial users in leasing the part of the foundry site parcel that Finkl purchased to protect itself from the expected influx of commercial or residential uses.

The 1988 Clybourn PMD regulations defined core and buffer areas for the district. When the district was adopted, the area designated as the core portion of the district was occupied predominantly by heavy manufacturing, with 100 percent industrial and manufacturing employment. In the section designated as the buffer area, there were more nonindustrial firms, but about 60 percent of the total employment was still industrial in nature. In its report recommending the Clybourn PMD, the Planning Department noted that the average wages for the industrial employees were more than twice that of the nonindustrial employees, and that tax revenues generated for the city by activities in this district were well over $1 million.

The Clybourn PMD regulations were designed to preserve this valuable manufacturing concentration. The principal features of the district's regulations are:

1. Prohibition of residential development throughout
   the district;
2. Only manufacturing and industrial uses to be permitted within the core area; and
3. Limitations on retail in the buffer area, including
   limited additional parking and a ban on drive-in or
   drive-through uses.

All parties got their piece of the pie with this solution: the industrial uses were protected from further encroachment, and
the nearby residential uses were protected from undesirable
commercial uses which were displacing the manufacturers.
The *Chicago Tribune* described the "Clybourn Experiment"
as: "Where grit meets glitz....The fit may not be perfect, but
the goal is to gentrify an urban wasteland without losing its
industrial muscle."[17]

Goose Island

Goose Island, situated in the north branch of the
Chicago River in the Near North River Corridor, was another
logical location for the PMD, but there the story has been
somewhat different. Described as a "feisty settlement of immigrants" that became a "district of tanners, smelters, and
manufacturers by the 20th century,"[18] Goose Island has remained a viable and active industrial area, providing over
2000 jobs in 1988.

Concern on Goose Island itself was ignited in 1986, when
a developer announced plans to reuse an empty Batchelder-
Beline Corporation scrap smelting plant just across the river
from Goose Island for an office-retail complex containing 250
"work-live" spaces, to be known as "River Lofts." Most of the
manufacturers on the Island opposed the rezoning, fearing
that their operations would be thrown into conflict with the
new residential uses especially. In the usual Chicago style,
there was considerable wheeling and dealing between the af-

fected parties. Finally, the Planning Department conducted meetings between the developer and the nearby manufacturers. The agreement that was finally reached:

1. Reduced the number of living units in the proposed River Lofts by half;
2. Provided that all commercial leases would contain a notification of the nearby manufacturing uses and a conflict resolution process;
3. Required the developer to fence, soundproof, etc. the project; and
4. Changed the rezoning classification which had previously been requested to reduce the impact of the City's performance standards.*

In addition, the Alderman agreed to PMD zoning for the Island, and the developer agreed not to develop additional property over which he had control on the Island for ten years unless in conformity with existing manufacturing zoning. The City agreed to install a cul-de-sac to more completely separate the manufacturing uses from the new development. This conflict, although resolved, appeared to be a harbinger of things to come; Goose Island seemed a logical choice for a PMD.

In its 1989 report recommending a PMD on Goose Island, the Planning Department found other pressures on manufacturing that warranted application of the PMD to this area. In one case, an industrial occupant that had rapidly expanded over recent years was unable to purchase additional land on the Island. In another case, even though the River Lofts project had not actually begun when the Planning Department prepared its report, one industrial user had already received a complaint about its operation, its first in its long history. Even more ominous for those who wished to preserve the manufacturing uses on the Island and ensure their viability was the reported acquisition of land on the Island by a commercial developer, who presumably had

---

*The degree of severity of the industrial performance standards is dependent upon the adjacent use; that is, if the adjacent use is residential, then the standard is more stringent than if the adjacent use is commercial.

no intent to preserve the noncommercial uses. Similar changes had been reported in the proposed "buffer" area, known as the Halsted Triangle, where many instances of conversion to commercial or retail space had occurred.

The proposed district would have applied to a 205-acre area that contained some firms that could not relocate to anywhere else in the Chicago area. The regulations proposed for the Goose Island district were similar in character to those adopted for Clybourn, though more detailed. Yet, in spite of the fact that application of the PMD to Goose Island appeared the logical next step, the Alderman for the area did not allow the district to be considered. It remains to be seen whether the district will be resurrected in the future and adopted to preserve the uses of this important area.

Conclusion

According to Gregory Longhini, Chicago's Planned Manufacturing District represents a "good compromise" for a difficult land-use problem. Such a long-standing policy debate preceded the district that, once adopted, the PMD became more than just another law. The real success of this district is that, in a city where zoning has often been up for grabs, this district is not. Longhini predicts that the district's status will not change for a long time—the PMD is a true consensus policy for the city, with the backing of the administration, the aldermen, and the citizens, a consensus that was created through long public debate. Others may not be so complimentary, citing unnecessary and unwarranted interference with the use of property—largely, one suspects, because the Chicago tradition of land speculation, zoning on demand, and unresponsive planning have been so firmly entrenched that it is difficult to conceive of any law that might be sacred. Because of this tradition, there is no risk in Chicago that "special district mania" will spoil zoning as usual in the city, even though another PMD is currently under serious consideration for an area adjacent to Clybourn. It is more likely that most zoning in Chicago will continue unaffected by this experiment.

Special Districts

An Evaluation

I think, based on New York's experience, special districts are the wave of the past.
    Howard Goldman, New York Zoning Attorney

Wave of the future...don't know another system that would create the kinds of responses to the needs of a fragile environment.
    Bruce Bonacker, Neighborhood Association
    President, San Francisco

I think special districts are one of the better things we do in this City....It was the best of our planning tools.
    Martin Gallent, New York Zoning Attorney

When we first sat down to evaluate the special district concept, we thought it would be a relatively simple matter to list the pros and cons of special districts and let each city decide whether or not it would choose to follow a similar path. However, each statement for or against special districts turns out to have an equally persuasive argument on the other side of the coin.

As with most modern policy issues, particularly in land use, it is absurd to even try to suggest a particular course that any given city should follow. There are too many subissues, including political ramifications, that are impossible to anticipate. Therefore, we have taken the easier way out in this evaluation; we will describe the principal issues related to special districts and let you decide.

Dealing with Complexity

Some proponents of special districts argue that a big city is too complex, each neighborhood too varied, to be handled in one generic zoning ordinance. It is essential to write "special" zoning provisions. We agree. The extreme complexity of our cities can not be questioned, and the special district concept has clearly provided a mechanism for addressing smaller areas within a city in a focused way.

Identifying What Is "Special"

Special districts seem to be in danger of overuse; they are often created for areas which may not really warrant "special" treatment. In reality, many of New York's special districts have few elements that are unusual compared to other parts of the city. Critics argue that special districts are created primarily for political reasons. This overuse of the designation is probably one of the principal reasons the present planning staff in New York is suspicious of special districts. Conn Howe, the Executive Director of the New York City Planning Commission, told us: "We were probably over-adventurous. We were calling [areas] special which really had no special aspects." Sandy Hornick added:

> We have to remember that there is the word "special" in special district and that you have to really ask yourself is what you are trying to accomplish really that special.

On the other hand, some areas really do merit special treatment. Perhaps the theater district was unique and required special rules not applicable to other areas of Manhattan. Moreover, it cannot be doubted that Clinton is a unique section of mid-Manhattan. Dismissing Clinton by saying that it is a political special district created to placate residents who feared the impact of a new convention center does not recognize the other forces at work in the area. Much, if not most, of American zoning is politically motivated, and truly appropriate special districts combine politics with genuine need.

Certainly the common problems of San Francisco's neighborhood commercial special districts—fast-food restaurants, large retailers, financial institutions, and the loss of second- and third-floor residential units—could have been treated through generic zoning. On the other hand, San Francisco has been able to hold the line at sixteen districts (compared to New York's thirty-seven), suggesting that planners there are successfully resisting calls for unnecessary districts.

Permanence

Once a special district has been created, it is very difficult to remove; special districts have proved to be very popular with the citizenry. The designation gives the residents a psychological lift, difficult to destroy even by earthquake. Clearly, most people would prefer to say that they live or work in the North Beach Neighborhood Commercial District or in the Special Clinton District than in an "R-4 west of 7th Avenue."

Every city that is considering using the special district technique should be aware of this risk: once started, special districting may be difficult to stop. Cities should ask themselves whether or not everyone with a land-use complaint will demand what amounts to a special zoning ordinance just for his or her area.

Administration

Perhaps the most serious problem with special districts is how difficult they are to administer. The original New York special districts were created under Mayor Lindsay in the 1960s by his new group of brilliant designers. These designers fashioned highly sophisticated and complex district provisions that had relatively few precise standards. Now Lindsay's designers are long-gone; the approval of a proposal is left to a skeptical Planning Commission, and the enforcement is left to a Building Department that can hardly be said to be staffed by persons trained in urban design. According to Sandy Hornick:

It was not just that they were urban designers, it was sort
of the best and the brightest. They were very bright. They
were going to come in and...solve all the city's ills...but they
came and they left. To some extent, they left behind things
which are too brilliant and complex to be administered by
people who are not brilliant and complex. It means that
you are going to fall considerably below the mark....That
essentially is what happened. They're administered by the
Building Department, which doesn't understand what
these special districts were supposed to accomplish in the
first place, but you're requiring a skilled level of plan ex-
aminers which they just aren't likely to have.

Perhaps we may be overstating this problem. After all,
many land-use regulations have been written by one group
and administered by another. Admittedly, the Urban Design
Group that Lindsay brought in was very special. Its members were talented, probably a bit too arrogant by half, and,
we suspect, not inclined to take suggestions. Their belief in
their own superiority hung on even after they departed; witness the incredible gobbledegook produced for the Special
Midtown District text—so incomprehensible it led Norman
Marcus to write a "translation" entitled "Plain English."

San Francisco has had a similar experience. Many of the
original architects of the special districts there are gone as
well, and a workload for the plan reviewers originally described as "crushing" must be indescribable at this point.

The inevitable result of not having regulations enforced
by those who have the greatest stake in them is a failure to
enforce them properly. The regulations are frequently left
completely impotent or in the hands of neighborhood vigi-
lantes. Overall, this situation is a recipe for chaos; when you
add to this a city administration that is uninterested in planning, the result is, well, a disaster.

Comprehensive Planning

Perhaps it is an overstatement to say that special districts are completely "anti-comprehensive planning," but

they often act as a substitute for it. New York's experience shows that the special district can be used as a way to avoid rewriting an entire zoning ordinance or doing any serious planning for the city as a whole. Undoubtedly, there would be a humongous effort and expense involved in rewriting New York's 1961 zoning ordinance. Victor Marrero, former Chairman of the Planning Commission, said that the Commission did toy with the idea of a rewrite:

> In fact, by the time I was in my second year at the Planning Commission, I came to the conclusion that it was timely to examine to what degree instead of doing all these things by special district and ad hoc, one shot at a time, we should be looking at it more generically and comprehensively. I began a study of the entire zoning resolution and created a zoning study group...to see whether we could cure the fact that, in just fifteen years under the 1961 zoning resolution, there were more amendments and exceptions than the total text of what existed in 1961.

And what came out of that effort? Another special district: Midtown. San Francisco came to the use of special districts in the opposite manner; its use actually grew out of a comprehensive revision to the entire zoning ordinance.

We suspect that, as cities attempt to deal with the increasingly specialized land-use needs of their citizens in an atmosphere of constrained budget and public resistance to change, special districts will be used as in New York to put off comprehensive reform. In New York City, no such major revision has occurred as yet, nor is it likely to have a high priority on subsequent City administration's list of things that must be done for the health and safety of its citizens.

The problem of comprehensive revision on a limited budget has no simple answer. The present squeeze on municipal finances and the drought in funds from the federal and state governments does not encourage municipalities to undertake such a revision program. Add to this the political turmoil that any comprehensive rewriting and remapping of the zoning ordinance would generate, and the task appears insurmountable. New York's zoning ordinance consists of hundreds of pages (three volumes), and it took almost ten years to complete the last major revision by 1961. Chicago's 1957 revision had taken only about three years to complete, but Chicago had the advantage of a Mayor who could easily push a revision through the most reluctant City Council once he was persuaded it was the best thing for the city.

Thus, special districts will probably continue to spread each time a problem is perceived in a particular area, such as the Bronx Grand Concourse or the Grand Central Terminal. After all, it is better to accomplish something for the city, even a small part, than to wait for years until the entire city can be replanned.

Spot Zoning

Special districts may also be a symptom of the failure of cities to comprehensively plan in the way that they may be used as a cover-up for "spot zoning." New York's Special Union Square District appears to be such a cover-up. As we detailed in Chapter 8, Zeckendorf wanted to build a high-rise condominium building that was not permitted under the generic zoning. Instead of rezoning his one parcel, the Planning Commission wrote special provisions for the entire area around Central Park that gave Zeckendorf what he wanted and deflected a charge of granting a special favor to one zoning lot. This trick sounds just like the current and prevalent perversions of Planned Development ordinances.

Neighborism

We have mentioned how dear special districts are to residents. There is no question that the very effort of formation has resulted in the knitting together of various interests in a prideful and positive way. There is, however, the inevitable negative side of this phenomenon. When a project is planned that is considered necessary for the city as a whole but that may adversely affect a special district, the district residents often will soundly resist it. We end up with a parochial clash between the city as a whole and the neighborhood and the special district. Rather than promoting the good of the entire city, the special district and its neighborhood associations frequently succumb to the NIMBY syndrome.

As Victor Marrero put it:

> You have to have a sense and an understanding of when issues transcend the boundaries of local interests and have citywide ramifications and implications. You have to have the strength and the judgment to put both interests on that scale and come out where you come out, bearing in mind that we are not the only participants in the process and that the ultimate result comes out from the continual participation of many other players in the "Zoning Game," and that total process sort of weeds out those where it is important to protect citywide interests and those elements where neighborhood interests prevail. We were there as key players but not necessarily the determinant forces in the game. It was just a matter again of having the balance and the strength to say no when it was appropriate to say no, and the will to do it when it had to be done in the face of opposition, whether it is from locals or from citywide interests. Sometimes it worked and sometimes it didn't.

Any city using special districts must recognize this issue and develop institutional mechanisms to deal with it. Perhaps New York's new charter provision regarding NIMBYs is a way to go. As we mentioned in Chapter 2, this provision requires the Planning Commission to adopt rules for the "fair distribution" of specified city facilities. Then in accordance with these rules, the Mayor is to establish an annual "statement of needs" on a citywide basis and designate sites for opening or expanding city facilities on the basis of the rules.

Inappropriate Purposes and Unforeseen Consequences

Two protests that are often heard about special districts are that they impose a burden of tasks on the zoning ordinance that it was never designed to achieve, and that often a district has consequences not intended by the framers. The latter complaint has merit—consider the fate of Yorkville (Chapter 8). The protest may be valid, but surely such errors are not the first time—nor the last—that planners and lawyers have suffered from astigmatism in land-use matters.

The charge that the special district tries to load the ordinance with functions not intended to be accomplished by zoning seems less persuasive. Yes, Clinton has a social purpose aside from urban design goals (and some of its provisions, such as the harassment provision, were badly drafted), but which municipality should cast the first stone in that regard? Zoning, almost from its conception and particularly in the suburbs, has often been used to advance social purposes. If Clinton and its lower-income residents can survive two decades longer than they would have without the special district, who is to say nay?

Critics often complain that special districts impose inappropriate economic—as well as social—burdens on zoning. Certainly, all of the neighborhood commercial special districts in San Francisco are open to this charge, as well as several New York districts. Is the Fifth Avenue Special District improperly trying to influence market forces by forbidding some uses the Planning Commission found objectionable (airline offices and branch banks)? If such uses represent the natural evolution of Fifth Avenue, critics ask, why should the City interfere? They have a plausible argument; yet what is wrong with a little market meddling in a good cause? Why should the City not try to protect the most famous shopping street in the world by keeping it the posh retail area it has been? In the case of the garment district, Southeast Asia may well take over all of the garment manufacturing for the United States, but why shouldn't New York City try to do something to deflect or retard the effects of these changes at home?

Negotiation and Bargaining

Perhaps the most invidious result of special districts is the element of negotiation and bargaining that accompanies their beginnings. "Let's make a deal" is the theme song. Under special districts, the tendency has been to negotiate each development approval application on a case-by-case basis. More "up front" standards in the ordinances would be helpful in some cases, but the drafters themselves are not always sure what these standards should be—witness the struggle in the theater district over how much of an FAR bonus should be given to a developer of a high rise for a theater in his building. Conn Howe acknowledged the danger:

> I think there is a lot of concern here, although frankly we haven't had any specific scandal, that there is a lot of concern about abuse, possible abuses, that even if you don't enter into a field of illegality, you at least have this problem where what you do one year for one development team, you do something different for a different development team the next year.

Another danger of the "conditional," "discretionary" review process is that it gives neighborhood advocates an incredible amount of potential power. One representative from a neighborhood association in San Francisco bragged about being able to stop most proposals; if the group did not object, the proposal would usually go right through. Under San Francisco's rules, all it takes is payment of a $50 filing fee by an objector to make a permitted use become discretionary, subject to hearings and all kinds of hazards. It is not surprising that representatives of developers advise their clients to take their investments elsewhere.

Conclusion and Recommendations

Where does all of this leave us? How can the chaos surrounding the creation and use of special zoning districts be controlled? Probably the only real solution is for the state government to reassert its latent power over planning and zoning and insist that every city have a plan and a zoning ordinance both consistent and in compliance with state policies. This would compel most of our cities to do the agonizing job of redrafting their plans and implementing regulations. But few states have the problems Florida has or the will Oregon mustered to pass legislation requiring comprehensive planning, and even in such states that have mandated this approach, the problems of compliance remain serious.

A possible compromise between comprehensive planning and the excessive use of special districts would be to insert procedural and substantive provisions regarding special districts into the zoning ordinance itself. This is currently being done in Chicago, Phoenix, and many parts of California. Such a section would alert the public to the possibility of creating a special district to address individual needs and yet clearly set out the "rules" governing such proposals. Those proposing a new special district should be required to demonstrate:

1. Why their area is unique;
2. Why the standard zoning provisions would not meet their needs, even if amended;
3. The extent of the support in their area for a special district and the nature of the opposition to the proposal;
4. The impacts on various citywide services and needs such as housing, transportation, and sewers; and
5. Why a more traditional historic district is not appropriate.

Requiring, in effect, the applicant to show why a generic approach to a problem area is not appropriate may focus the attention of those proposing and evaluating the district— thereby, perhaps, minimizing special district proliferation.

Special districts are no better nor worse than any other land-use regulatory technique. They offer short-term solutions usually for the long-term. They have fostered community pride often at the expense of citywide solutions. They have usually been more successful preserving a particular status quo, rather than encouraging development. Nevertheless, Victor Marrero asserts:

> I think that the use of the special district to encourage development could be as important as that of preserva-

tion. Here [in New York], it has been used for both purposes, in some cases successfully and in other not successfully, but the fact is that it is available to both.

To say that they are the "wave of the future" may be accurate
but also sad. We can cautiously recommend them for cities
that cannot effectively address citywide problems in the fore-
seeable future.

Notes

Chapter 1: Prologue

1. Douglas Porter, "On Bemoaning Zoning," *Urban Land* (March 1983): 34.

2. *Village of Euclid v. Ambler Realty Corp.*, 272 U.S. 365 (1926).

3. *Asian Americans for Equality v. Koch*, 72 N.Y. 2d 121, 531 NYS 2d 782, 786 (1988).

Chapter 2: The Players

1. The City of New York's 1982 Request For Proposal for the Coliseum site, cited in *Harvard Journal of Public Policy*, (Summer-Fall 1985): 35.

2. Sydney Schanberg, *Newsday*, 2 February 1987. A Newsday quote reprinted and distributed by the Lincoln Institute of Land Policy. Newsday, Inc., Copyright 1987.

3. Ibid. A Newsday quote reprinted and distributed by the Lincoln Institute of Land Policy. Newsday, Inc., Copyright 1987.

4. Paul Goldberger, "Architecture View; Square Deal for Columbus Circle?" *New York Times*, 18 October 1987, Sect. 2, 1. Copyright © 1987 by The New York Times Company. Reprinted by permission.

5. Mortimer B. Zuckerman, quoted in Mark McCain, "All Is Far From Quiet on the Western Front," *New York Times*, 11 October 1987. Copyright © 1987 by The New York Times Company. Reprinted by permission.

6. *Municipal Art Society et al. v. City of New York, et al.*, 137 Misc. 2d 832, 522 N.Y.S. 800 (S. Ct. 1987).

7. Sydney Schanberg, Editorial, *Newsday*, 9 December 1987. A Newsday quote reprinted and distributed by the Lincoln Institute of Land Policy. Newsday, Inc., Copyright 1987.

8. Paul Goldberger, *New York Times*, 19 June 1988.

9. *Municipal Art Society, et al. v. New York City*, City's Brief on Appeal (1988) at 2.

10. John E. Zuccotti, letter to Richard F. Babcock, 16 May 1990. Reprinted by permission.

11. David Dinkins, speech before the Municipal Art Society, 12 July 1989.

12. *Board of Estimate of City of New York v. Morris*, 109 S.Ct. 1433 (1989).

13. Timothy Bradley, "Charter Revision: Land Use Compromises," *The Livable City* (New York: Municipal Art Society, October 1989), 7. Reprinted by permission.

14. Ibid.

15. Ibid.

Chapter 3: The Theater District

1. Memorandum of law for Landmarks Preservation Commission in *The Shubert Organization, Inc., et al. v. Landmarks Preservation Commission of the City of New York*, Supreme Court of New York, Index No. 12587/88.

2. Brendan Gill, "The Sky Line: On the Brink," *New Yorker*, 9 November 1987, 116. Reprinted by permission; © 1987 Brendan Gill. Originally in the *New Yorker*.

3. Ibid. Reprinted by permission; © 1987 Brendan Gill. Originally in the *New Yorker*.

4. Jonathan Barnett, *Urban Design as Public Policy* (New York: Architectural Record, 1974), 17.

5. Ibid.

6. Mayor Lindsay's words related by Donald Elliott in interview 13 March 1987.

7. New York City Planning Commission, Department of City Planning, *Midtown Zoning*, New York, N.Y., March 1982, 224, S. 81-742.

8. Gill, 116. Reprinted by permission; © 1987 Brendan Gill. Originally in the *New Yorker*.

9. Ada Louise Huxtable, "Architecture/Design; Creeping Gigantism in Manhattan," *New York Times*, 22 March 1987, Sec. 2, 1. Copyright © 1987 by The New York Times Company. Reprinted by permission.

10. Ibid. Copyright © 1987 by The New York Times Company. Reprinted by permission.

11. Paul Goldberger, "The New Times Square Design: Merely Token Changes," *New York Times*, 1 September 1989, Sect. B, 1. Copyright © 1989 by The New York Times Company. Reprinted by permission.

12. Ibid. Copyright © 1989 by The New York Times Company. Reprinted by permission.

13. Jonathan Barnett, *An Introduction to Urban Design* (New York: Harper & Row Publishers, 1982), 99.

Chapter 4: Clinton

1. Weiner/Gran Associates, *Clinton: A Plan for Preservation*, report prepared for the Clinton Steering Committee and the New York Department of City Planning, 1974, 4.

2. Ibid., 4.

3. Barbara Lippman, "Harassment Law Voided: Not Constitutional, U.S. Judge Decides," *New York Daily News*, 2 March 1987. Reprinted by permission.

4. New York City Planning Commission, report on "The Establishment of a New Special Clinton Interim Preservation District," CP-22436, 7 November 1973.

5. City of New York, Special Clinton District Ordinance, Article IX, Chapter 6, Section 96.00, "General Purposes."

6. City of New York, Special Clinton District Ordinance, Article IX, Chapter 6, Section 96.109 (b).

7. *ABN 51st Street Partners v. City of New York*, 724 F.Supp. 1142 (S.D. NY 1989).

8. Ibid.

Chapter 5: Fifth Avenue and Little Italy

1. Seymour Toll, *Zoned American* (New York: Grossman Publishers, 1969), 77.

2. New School of Social Research, *The Special District Zoning Concept in New York City*, report by the Department of Urban Affairs & Policy Analysis, Center for New York City Affairs, 1975, 16.

3. Office of Midtown Planning Department, report to the New York City Planning Commission, 1971.

4. New School of Social Research, 17.

5. New York City Planning Commission, resolution recommending a Special Fifth Avenue District, 3 March 1971.

6. City of New York, Special Fifth Avenue District Ordinance, 87.00-87.12.

7. New School of Social Research, 80.

8. Raquel Ramati, *How To Save Your Own Street* (Garden City, NY: Doubleday and Company, 1981), 60, 62.

9. Ramati, 72.

10. New York City Planning Commission, Minutes of meeting 5 January 1977, 1.

Chapter 6: Midtown

1. New York City Planning Commission, Department of City Planning, *Midtown Zoning*, March 1982, 9-10.

2. New York City Planning Commission, *Midtown Zoning*, 11.

3. New York City Planning Commission, *Midtown Development Review*, July 1987, 3.

4. John Taylor, "Pushing the Outer Limits," *New York Magazine*, 10 April 1989. All of the quotations and information presented in this section are taken from this article. Copyright © 1990 News America Publishing, Inc. All rights reserved. Reprinted with the permission of *New York Magazine*.

Chapter 7: The Garment District

1. Affidavit of Richard Satkin in December 1987 at 3, *Real Estate Board of New York, Inc., et al. v. City of New York et al.*, Index No. 17462/87 (Sup. Ct.: New York County).

2. Ibid., 11.

3. Affidavit of William G. Conway on March 1, 1988 at 8, *Real Estate Board of New York, Inc., et al. v. City of New York et al.*, Index No. 17462/87 (Sup. Ct: New York County).

4. *Real Estate Board of New York, Inc. et al. v. City of New York et al.*, Supreme Court: New York County, Index No. 17462/87.

5. Slip Opinion, at 2.

Chapter 8: The Importance of Being Special

1. New York City Planning Commission, Minutes of meeting 3 April 1974.

2. New York Department of City Planning, *Grand Concourse: Special Zoning District Proposal*, April 1986, 6.

3. Ibid., 7.

4. Ibid., 29.

5. Ibid., 32-33.

6. Ibid., 36.

7. New York City Planning Commission, *Grand Central Area: Proposal for a Special Sub-District*, report to the New York City Board of Estimate, November 1989, 4.

8. Ibid.

Chapter 10: Chicago

1. R. Giloth and J. Betancur, "Where Downtown Meets Neighborhood: Industrial Displacement in Chicago, 1978-1987," *Journal of the American Planning Association* (Summer 1988): 280.

2. Giloth and Betancur, 280, give the figure as nearly 100,000. D. Allardice, W. Wiewel, and W. Wintermute, "The Strength of Size and Diversity Changes in the Chicago Economy, 1979-1986," paper presented at Great Lakes Conference 4 (August 23, 1989), 4, note a 17% decline in manufacturing jobs, or over 144,000 jobs.

3. Corporate Realty Advisors, Inc., "The CRA Report: Chicago Area Industrial Survey 1982-88," Chicago, 1988. Figures compiled on basis of quarterly report of available industrial space in Chicago.

4. Giloth and Betancur, 281.

5. Allardice et al., 4.

6. Ibid., 283.

7. Giloth and Betancur, 285.

8. Chicago Association of Neighborhood Development Organizations and Siemon, Larsen & Purdy, "Land Use Techniques for Industrial Preservation, A Report to the National Trust for Historic Preservation," 1988, 62. This source referred to as CANDO in subsequent notes.

9. Ibid., 58.

10. Connie Lauerman, "The Clybourn Experiment," *Chicago Tribune Magazine* (18 February 1990): 14, col. 1.

11. Ibid., 15, col. 1.

12. Ibid., 17, col. 1.

13. CANDO, 1.

14. Giloth and Betancur, 285. Reprinted by permission of the *Journal of the American Planning Association*.

15. CANDO, Appendix B, "Agreement for Link Development Between Centmon Properties, Inc. and City of Chicago," 2.

16. Ibid, 4.

17. Lauerman, 13-14.

18. Giloth and Betancur, 286. Reprinted by permission of the *Journal of the American Planning Association*.

Appendix A

Special Zoning Districts

The most widely used affirmative zoning technique is special district zoning. This technique permits areas with unique characteristics to flourish rather than be overwhelmed by standard development. The Commission has established special zoning districts to achieve specific planning and urban design objectives in a limited area. Each district stipulates requirements and/or provides zoning incentives for developers who provide the specific urban qualities the Commission seeks to promote in that area. It is a way of using private capital to carry out public policy. A brief description of the intent of each district is given below:

Special Midtown District (Manhattan)

The Special Midtown District was established to guide all development within the midtown central business district. Included within the special district are three areas of special concern that are subject to additional regulations. These subdistricts are: the Theater District, the Preservation Subdistrict and the Fifth Avenue Subdistrict.

The Special Midtown District has a base FAR of 15.0 along avenue frontages and an FAR of 12.0 in the midblocks. The base FAR in the Preservation Subdistrict is 8.0 in order to restrict development on the side streets surrounding the Mu-

Source: New York City Department of City Planning, *Zoning Handbook*, 1988, 89-95. Author's Note: the Special Grand Concourse District was established too recently to be included in this 1988 listing.

seum of Modern Art. The base FAR of the Theater Subdistrict core (on Broadway and Seventh Avenue frontages around Times Square) is set at 14.0 FAR, the FAR in the midblocks between Sixth and Seventh avenues is set at 12.0 and the FAR in the midblocks between Broadway and Eighth Avenue is 10.0.

The core of the Theater Subdistrict has the highest concentration of legitimate theaters and entertainment-related uses. The Theater Subdistrict text requires a City Planning Commission special permit for demolition of any of the 44 legitimate theaters that are not designated landmarks.

The Theater Subdistrict has special use and signage requirements (in keeping with the character of the area). A flexible development rights transfer provision has been established for the preservation of landmark theaters. In the Theater Subdistrict, a new building above a certain size must reserve at least 5 percent of its floor space (not FAR) for entertainment and theater-related uses. Areas located outside the Preservation Subdistrict and the Theater Subdistrict are eligible for an as-of-right FAR bonus for urban plazas, through-block galleries and theater retention. The only bonus available in the Theater Subdistrict core is the City Planning Commission special permit bonus for rehabilitation of listed theaters. The Preservation Subdistrict is not eligible for any floor area bonus. Other remaining areas can receive a floor area bonus for subway station improvements and for rehabilitation of theaters.

Certain urban design features, such as continuity of street wall and retail uses, off-street relocation of existing subway stairs, and provision of on-site pedestrian circulation spaces are mandated. The special district also includes certain use and signage controls for the Fifth Avenue and theater subdistricts. Special daylight evaluation criteria are included to ensure the availability of light and air on midtown streets. The midtown district represents a shift away from discretionary zoning to more predictable, as-of-right development.

Special Lincoln Square District (Manhattan)

The Special Lincoln Square District was established to enhance the character of the area surrounding Lincoln Square as an international center for the performing arts. The district mandates the height of building walls along certain streets and the placement of arcades and types of commercial use at street level as a means of guiding the orderly redevelopment of the Lincoln Square area. The district accomplishes its objectives by offering special floor area bonuses by special permit from the Planning Commission and the Board of Estimate for new development that includes the following public amenities: mandatory arcades, subsurface concourse connections to subways or subway improvements, and lower-income housing as set forth in the provisions of Inclusionary Housing.

Special Limited Commercial District (Manhattan)

The Special Limited Commercial District attempts to preserve the character of commercial areas within historic districts by restricting commercial uses to those uses compatible with the historic district, and by mandating that all commercial uses be in completely enclosed buildings. In addition, limitations are also set for the size and illumination of signs within the special district. One such special district has been mapped in Greenwich Village.

Special Battery Park City District (Manhattan)

The Special Battery Park City District was created to govern extensive residential and commercial development in an area close to the business core of Lower Manhattan in accordance with a master plan for Battery Park City.

The centerpiece of the master plan is the office complex. To the north and south of this complex are two large residential neighborhoods with street-level retail uses. One major element of the plan is a continuous esplanade providing public access to the Hudson River waterfront. The district contains

special design controls with respect to floor area ratio, required building walls and permissible building height.

Special United Nations
Development District (Manhattan)

The Special United Nations Development District attempts
to guide the development of the midtown area adjacent to the
United Nations. A major feature of the development proposal
is a unified design concept. The basic floor area ratio for the
district was increased from 10.0 to 15.0 to promote special
public amenities needed in the area and to implement the
development plan.

Special Greenwich Street
Development District (Manhattan)

The special Greenwich Street Development District was established to foster and promote the orderly expansion of commercial development in an area of Lower Manhattan adjacent to Battery Park City and the World Trade Center.

This district attempts to implement an integrated plan for
improved pedestrian and vehicular circulation and to encourage development of a variety of retail and service establishments to meet the needs of the area's working population.
This is accomplished through a series of pedestrian circulation and lot improvements relating to each property in the
district for which floor area bonuses are offered.

Some unique features of this district are its provisions for
involving both the developer and appropriate public agencies in the construction of certain pedestrian circulation improvements.

Special South Street Seaport District (Manhattan)

The purpose of the Special South Street Seaport District is to
facilitate the preservation and restoration of the seaport's

historic buildings in accordance with an approved development plan. The low scale of the seaport is retained by transferring development rights above the low buildings to specified neighboring locations for commercial development.

Special Manhattan Landing Development District

The Special Manhattan Landing Development District guides off-shore development from Battery Park to the Manhattan Bridge along the East River. This district is under review.

Special Lower Manhattan Mixed Use District

The Special Lower Manhattan Mixed Use District was enacted to permit limited residential development in an otherwise industrial 62-block area in Manhattan south of Canal Street. That portion of the district which is mapped as an overlay on existing manufacturing zones permits certain older manufacturing buildings to be converted to loft dwellings and joint living-work quarters for artists. Where the district is mapped as an overlay on existing commercial zones, new contextual residential development is permitted. At the same time, retention of the underlying zoning protects the economic vitality of this area.

Special Park Improvement District (Manhattan)

The Special Park Improvement District was created to preserve the character and architectural quality of Fifth and Park Avenues. It limits the height of new buildings to 210 feet or 19 stories, whichever is less, and mandates streetwall continuity.

Special Clinton District (Manhattan)

The Special Clinton District in Manhattan was created to ensure that the Clinton community is not adversely affected by new development. Its provisions are under review.

Special Sheepshead Bay District (Brooklyn)

The Special Sheepshead Bay District was devised to encourage development that will strengthen and protect the neighborhood's unique waterfront recreation and commercial character. In the area immediately north of the fishing fleet wharves, commercial uses are restricted to uses that support waterfront and tourist-related activities.

All new development along Emmons Avenue must provide widened sidewalks, street trees, and plazas which may contain sitting areas, landscaping, kiosks and cafes. Floor area bonuses are provided for plazas, arcades, usable residential open space and additional accessory commercial parking. Special density and height limits have been established.

Special Northside Mixed Use District (Brooklyn)

This mixed use district is designed to meet the needs of a neighborhood where housing and industry co-exist. The Commission selectively mapped mixed use areas—R(M) when the area is primarily residential and M(R) when it is industrial—to allow controlled residential or light manufacturing expansion where such uses can grow and function without conflict.

R(M) and M(R) districts combine the regulations for R6 and M1 areas. In an M(R) district, manufacturing uses are permitted to develop in the same manner as in any other M1 district. Existing residences may be enlarged and new residential construction is permitted as-of-right on blocks that are already primarily residential. New residential construction is permitted on certain other sites after approval of a special permit by the City Planning Commission and the Board of Estimate.

In an R(M) district, residential uses are permitted to develop in the same manner as in any other R6 district. Limited expansion of selected light industries that do not conflict with residential uses is permitted. Other industries become nonconforming and are allowed to remain but not to expand. New industrial development requires a special permit from the City Planning Commission and the Board of Estimate.

Special Madison Avenue Preservation District (Manhattan)

The Special Madison Avenue Preservation District is intended to preserve and reinforce the unique character of Madison Avenue and the surrounding area (from 61st to 96th Streets). Bulk and street wall height provisions limit the height of new development to the scale of existing buildings and require a continuous building facade along Madison Avenue, mandate continuous ground floor development of a selected list of appropriate shops, and require the provision of usable recreation space at rooftop levels. Within this district the maximum permissible floor area ratio is 10. Since building height is limited, greater building coverage is allowed.

Special Transit Land Use District (Manhattan)

The Special Transit Land Use District relates development along Second Avenue to a future subway line. The special district requires builders of developments adjoining subway stations to reserve space in their projects, by providing an easement, for public access to the subway or other subway-related use. The resulting new subway entrances and mezzanines would be airy, attractive and functional instead of sidewalk obstructions that impede pedestrian circulation. The district is mapped at locations between Chatham Square and East 126th Street.

Special Yorkville-East 86th Street District (Manhattan)

The Special Yorkville-East 86th Street District attempts to preserve and strengthen the unique commercial and residential character of the neighborhood by restricting the construction of office buildings and department stores, mandating the construction of buildings to the existing street line, and reserving ground floor space for restaurants and a wide variety of shops and commercial uses characteristic of the area. Floor area bonuses are allowed only when floor area is reserved for housing for the elderly or where small public parks are provided in certain portions of the special district. The district requires roof gardens, street trees and improved pedestrian circulation around subway stations. This district is under review.

Special Atlantic Avenue District (Brooklyn)

The Special Atlantic Avenue District was created to preserve the scale and character of Atlantic Avenue, including certain architectural features of the buildings. The special district provides flexibility in arranging building bulk, mandates street level commercial uses and establishes design guidelines for renovation and new construction. Demolition of buildings is prohibited in the district except in the case of unsafe buildings, or to make way for a new development for which a building permit and financial commitments have been secured. To improve the visual character of the avenue, special sign regulations are imposed for commercial establishments.

Special Planned Community Preservation District (Manhattan, Queens, the Bronx)

The Special Planned Community Preservation District designation protects the unique character of well-planned communities that have been developed as a unit. Those communities characteristically have large landscaped open spaces and a superior relationship of buildings, open spaces, commercial uses, and pedestrian and vehicular circulation. In many cases, they have been threatened by development pressures. No demolition, new development, enlargement or alteration of landscaping or topography is permitted within the district except by special permit of the City Planning Commission and the Board of Estimate. Preservation districts have been mapped in Sunnyside Gardens, Fresh Meadows, Parkchester and Harlem River Houses.

Special Scenic View District (Brooklyn)

The Special Scenic View District is intended to prevent ob-
struction of outstanding scenic views as seen from a public
park, esplanade or mapped public place. No buildings or structures are allowed to penetrate a scenic view plane except by
special permit of the City Planning Commission and the Board
of Estimate. To protect the waterfront view of the Lower Manhattan skyline, Governor's Island, the Statue of Liberty and
the Brooklyn Bridge, a special scenic view district has been
mapped for the area west of the Brooklyn Heights Esplanade.

Special Natural Area District
(Queens, the Bronx, Staten Island)

The purpose of the Special Natural Area District is to preserve unique natural characteristics, such as aquatic, bio-
logic, geologic and topographic features having ecological and
conservation values, by reviewing all new developments and
site alterations on primarily vacant land. Natural features
are protected by limiting modifications in topography, by preserving tree, plant and marine life, and natural water
courses, and by requiring clustered development to maximize
the preservation of natural features.

Under the regulations of the special district, the City Planning Commission must certify that all new development in
mapped natural area districts meets applicable preservation standards.

Special natural area districts have been mapped in the Green-
belt and Von Briesen Park areas of Staten Island, in Riverdale
and in Fort Totten. These areas are endowed with steep slopes,
rock outcrops, creeks, and a variety of botanic environments.

The Special Coney Island Mixed Use District (Brooklyn)

The Special Coney Island Mixed Use District was established
to stabilize residential development while protecting the
area's industrial base.

The district allows limited new residential infill and requires special permits for large new industrial developments. Existing residential buildings are allowed enlargements, alterations and repairs, and construction of new residential buildings is allowed if the buildings are next to an existing residential or community facility use.

New manufacturing is limited to certain light industries compatible with residential uses.

Special South Richmond Development District (Staten Island)

The Special South Richmond Development District was established to guide development of predominantly vacant land in the southern half of Staten Island. The special district maintains the densities established by the underlying zones and ensures that new development is compatible with existing communities.

To maintain the existing community character, the district mandates tree preservation, planting requirements, controls on changes to the topography, height limits, and setback and curb cut restrictions along railroads and certain roads. It restricts construction within designated open space (a defined network of open space set aside for preservation in its natural state). To preserve designated open space without penalizing the owner of such space, the owner is permitted to transfer development rights from the designated open space to the balance of his property.

A topographic survey and a report on the availability of public services must be submitted by the developer as a prerequisite to any application for development. A performance bond must also be provided to assure continued maintenance and improvement of public open space. The open space provisions are currently under review.

The Special Franklin Street
Mixed Use District (Brooklyn)

The Special Franklin Street Mixed Use District was established to achieve a balance between residential and industrial uses by remapping the area from an M1-1 district to an R6(M-1) district. The district allows residential and community facility uses according to R6 district regulations. All existing industrial uses may expand by 3,000 square feet, or 50 percent, whichever is less. A larger expansion may be granted by special permit from the City Planning Commission.

A new Use Group, Use Group M, has been established which allows light industries and commercial uses in Use Groups 6, 7, 9 and 11 to occupy vacant storefronts.

Special Little Italy District (Manhattan)

The Special Little Italy District was established to preserve and enhance the historic and commercial character of this community. Special use regulations protect the retail area along Mulberry Street. Other regulations encourage residential rehabilitation and new development on a scale consistent with existing buildings, discourage the demolition of noteworthy buildings, and increase the number of street trees in the area.

Special City Island District (the Bronx)

The Special City Island District was adopted to preserve the nautical uses and low-rise residential character of City Island. The special district regulations restrict the size and illumination of business signs and limit building heights to three to five stories and ensure adequate parking. The only commercial and manufacturing uses permitted are those which reflect the nautical flavor of the island or serve the retail needs of the residents.

Special Ocean Parkway District (Brooklyn)

The purpose of the Special Ocean Parkway District is to strengthen the existing character and quality of the community and to enhance the scenic landmark designation of Ocean Parkway in Brooklyn. All new community facility developments or enlargements are limited except by special permission to the residential bulk regulations of the underlying districts. All developments with frontage on Ocean Parkway are required to provide a 30-foot unobstructed front yard, subject to limitations on paving and landscaping, thereby preserving the character envisioned by the original designer of the parkway. Accessory off-street parking for all new developments must be completely enclosed and all new developments along Ocean Parkway are required to provide street trees.

Special Bay Ridge District (Brooklyn)

The Special Bay Ridge District was established to protect the existing scale and character of the Bay Ridge community. The special district distinguishes the scale of development in the midblock from that on the avenue frontage. The midblock street zone encourages two- and three-family homes with a maximum height of three stories. The avenue zone encourages the rehabilitation of existing structures and limits new development to a six to eight story maximum. Special setbacks, curb cuts, open space, tree planting and ground floor commercial requirements have been included to preserve the character of the existing street wall both along the avenues and side streets.

Special Fulton Mall District (Brooklyn)

The Special Fulton Mall District in Downtown Brooklyn was established to create an attractive shopping environment as part of a city street mall plan. Special retail use, sign, facade and circulation improvement regulations are provided. A special assessment district has been created, through state legislation, to maintain the mall.

Vehicular traffic (except buses) is prohibited within the mall. Major public amenities required within the district include: improved transit access, street furniture, street lighting, tree planting and special treatment of the sidewalks and roadbeds.

Special Hunters Point Mixed Use District (Queens)

The Special Hunters Point Mixed Use District was created to permit limited as-of-right status for the enlargement/alteration of existing residential buildings and for new infill residential construction. All residential and community facility uses are subject to R5 district regulations. In some cases, a special permit is required for certain residential and community facility uses. New manufacturing and commercial uses, or enlargement of existing buildings containing such uses, are allowed as-of-right as long as these developments or enlargements contain no residential uses and do not cause significant adverse environmental impacts. Such new developments or enlargements must meet M1 district performance standards.

The Special Court Square Subdistrict has been created within this special district to encourage high density commercial development in an area well-served by the subway system.

Special Union Square District (Manhattan)

The Special Union Square District was established to revitalize the area around Union Square by encouraging mixed use development. Its urban design provisions are designed to provide compatibility between new development, existing buildings and Union Square Park. The district mandates ground floor retail uses, off-street relocation of subway stairs and the continuity of street walls. Special streetscape and signage controls enhance the physical appearance of the district. Within this district a floor area ratio bonus for subway improvements is available by special permit.

Special Manhattan Bridge District

The Special Manhattan Bridge District was established to preserve the residential character of this Lower Manhattan community, to minimize residential relocation on development sites and to provide for selective demolition and rehabilitation of existing buildings. A special floor area bonus is allowed for the provision of new community facility space and/or dwelling units for low- and moderate-income families. Within this district it is possible to transfer development rights from a site containing existing buildings to a new development. The district mandates that street trees be planted in connection with a new development.

Special Hillside Preservation District (Staten Island)

The purpose of the Special Hillside Preservation District is to preserve the hilly terrain and unique natural features of Staten Island by reducing hillside erosion, landslides and excessive stormwater runoff. The primary concept for regulating development under this special district is the slope coverage approach: As the development site becomes steeper, the permitted building coverage decreases, but the permissible floor area on the site remains the same.

Special Garment Center District (Manhattan)

The Special Garment Center District was created to maintain the viability of apparel production in selected midblocks in the city's Garment Center by creating a preservation area within which the conversion of manufacturing space to office use is restricted. Conversion to office use in the preservation area is permitted only by certification of the City Planning Commission that an equal amount of comparable floor area has been preserved for specific manufacturing uses. The legality of this special district is currently being litigated.

Appendix B

Listed Theaters:
Special Midtown District

Theater Name	Address	Block Number	Lot Number
Alvin	250 West 52nd Street	1023	54
Ambassador	215 West 49th Street	1021	15
ANTA	245 West 52nd Street	1024	7
Barrymore	243 West 47th Street	1019	12
Belasco	111 West 44th Street	997	23
Biltmore	261 West 47th Street	1019	5
Booth	222 West 45th Street	1016	15
Broadhurst	235 West 44th Street	1016	11
Broadway	1681 Broadway	1024	46
Brooks Atkinson	256 West 47th Street	1018	57
City Center	131 West 55th Street	1008	15
Cort	138 West 48th Street	1000	49
Ed Sullivan	1697 Broadway	1025	43
Eugene O'Neill	230 West 49th Street	1020	53
Forty-Sixth Street	226 West 46th Street	1017	48
Golden	252 West 45th Street	1016	58
Harris	226 West 42nd Street	1013	45
Henry W. Miller	124 West 43rd Street	995	45
Hudson	139 West 44th Street	997	15
Imperial	249 West 45th Street	1017	10
Liberty	234 West 42nd Street	1013	49
Little	240 West 44th Street	1015	51
Longacre	220 West 48th Street	1019	50
Lunt-Fontanne	205 West 46th Street	1018	20

Source: New York City Planning Commission, Department of City Planning, *Midtown Zoning*, March 1982, 225-226, S. 81-742.

Theater Name	Address	Block Number	Lot Number
Lyceum	149 West 45th Street	998	8
Lyric	213 West 42nd Street	1014	39
Majestic	245 West 44th Street	1016	5
Mark Hellinger	237 West 51st Street	1023	11
Music Box	239 West 45th Street	1017	11
Nederlander	208 West 41st Street	1012	30
New Amsterdam	214 West 42nd Street	1013	39
New Amsterdam Roof Garden	214 West 42nd Street	1013	39
New Apollo	234 West 43rd Street	1014	20
Palace	1564 Broadway	999	63
Plymouth	236 West 45th Street	1016	51
R.F.K.	225 West 48th Street	1020	14
Royale	242 West 45th Street	1016	55
St. James	246 West 44th Street	1015	54
Selwyn	229 West 42nd Street	1014	17
Shubert	225 West 44th Street	1016	15
Studio 54	254 West 54th Street	1025	58
Times Square	219 West 42nd Street	1014	20
Victory	209 West 42nd Street	1014	25
Winter Garden	1634 Broadway	1022	2

Appendix C

Special Regulations for Fifth Avenue Subdistrict

81-81
General Provisions
The regulations of Sections 81-82 to 81-84, inclusive, relating to Special Regulations for Fifth Avenue Subdistrict are applicable only in the Fifth Avenue Subdistrict....They supplement or modify the regulations of this Chapter applying generally to the *Special Midtown District*, of which this Subdistrict is a part.

81-82
Special Regulations on Permitted and Required Uses
In order to insure the continued development and stability of department stores, specialty stores, boutiques and international stores, the following special limitations are imposed on the location and kinds of *uses* and *signs* permitted within the Fifth Avenue Subdistrict. These requirements and limitations shall apply to *developments, enlargements, extensions* or changes of *use*.
    (a) Restriction on ground floor *uses*
        For any *developments* located within the Fifth Avenue Subdistrict, *uses* located on the ground floor level or within five feet of *curb level*, except for lobby space, shall be limited to retail *uses* listed in Use Group F. This restriction shall not apply to *uses* permitted in

Source: New York City Planning Commission, Department of City Planning, *Midtown Zoning*, March 1982, 239,241,243, S. 81-80 to 81-84.

the underlying district for which valid leases were executed prior to March 25, 1971, and to which a member of the bar of the State of New York shall attest.

(b) Minimum retail space requirement

Any *development* or portion thereof located within the Fifth Avenue Subdistrict shall contain *uses* listed in Use Group F with a *floor area ratio* of not less than 1.0. When existing *uses* listed in Use Group F are retained within a *development* or *enlargement*, their *floor area* may be counted toward such requirement. In order to count toward the requirement, retail or service establishments shall be located on levels up to but not exceeding a height of six *stories* or 85 feet, whichever is less, or not more than five feet below *curb level*.

(c) Use Group F

Use Group F comprises a group of retail establishments selected to promote and strengthen retail business in the Fifty Avenue Subdistrict.

Antique stores

Art galleries, *commercial*

Artists' supply stores

* Banks

Beauty parlors

Book or card stores

Candy stores

Clothing or clothing accessory stores, with no limitation on *floor area* per establishment

Department stores

Eating or drinking places, including those which provide outdoor table service or incidental musical entertainment either by mechanical device or by not more than three persons playing piano, organ, accordion, guitar, or any stringed instrument

Florist shops

Food stores, including supermarkets, grocery stores, meat markets, or delicatessen stores

Furrier shops, custom

Gift shops

Jewelry shops

Leather goods or luggage stores
Millinery shops
Music shops
Newsstands, open or enclosed
Optician or optometrist establishments
Package liquor stores
Photograph equipment or supply stores
Record shops
Shoe stores
Sporting or athletic stores
Stamp or coin stores
Stationery stores
Tailor or dressmaking shops, custom
Television, radio, phonograph or household appliance
   stores
Toy stores
* Travel bureaus
Variety stores
Watch or clock stores or repair shops

> * any *use* or uses marked with an asterisk shall occupy in the aggregate at the ground floor level no more than 15 percent of the linear *street* frontage of the *zoning lot* on or within 50 feet of Fifth Avenue and no more than 10 percent of the total *lot area* of the *zoning lot* within 50 feet of Fifth Avenue.

(d) Modifications of *use* regulations on *zoning lot* with no frontage on Fifth Avenue

For a *zoning lot* which has no frontage on Fifth Avenue, the mandatory retail *use* regulations of this Section may be modified for that portion of the *zoning lot* located more than 100 feet from the *street line* of Fifth Avenue, provided that the City Planning Commission certifies that the ground floor space is occupied by a *community facility use* which maintains front wall transparency up to a height of one *story* above the abutting sidewalk level generating pedestrian interest and activity, and is compatible with the character and objectives of the Fifth Avenue Subdistrict. In no event shall the *street line* frontage occupied by such *use* exceed 30 feet.

(e) The following special *sign* regulations apply to existing as well as new establishments or *uses*.

(1) The aggregate area of all *signs* in ground floor store windows is restricted to not more than one-third of the window area.

(2) The display of banners or pennants from the exteriors of *buildings* is prohibited.

81-83
Special Street Wall Requirements

The *street wall* of any *building* with frontage on Fifth Avenue shall extend without setback from the Fifth Avenue *street line* for at least 90 percent of the entire length of the *front lot line*. The *street wall* shall reach a minimum required height of 85 feet and shall not exceed a height of 125 feet at or within 10 feet of the *street line*.

Where a new *development* or *enlargement* occupies less than an entire *block* front of Fifth Avenue frontage, the height of the *street wall* at the *street line* shall be not more than 10 feet above or below the height of the adjacent existing *building* at the *street line*. If the new *development* or *enlargement* is on an *interior lot* between two existing adjacent *buildings* of different heights, the height of the new *development* or *enlargement's street wall* at the *street line* shall be not more than 10 feet above or below the *street wall* height of one of the adjacent *buildings* at the *street line*. However, this shall not be construed to permit a *street wall* height of less than 85 feet or more than 125 feet at the *street line*.

For the purpose of calculating the maximum *street wall* height on the *narrow street* frontage of a *corner lot* by the weighted average method, as set forth in paragraph (b) of Section 81-262 (Maximum height of front wall at the street line), the maximum *street wall* height generally applicable along the *narrow street* shall be averaged with a height of 150 feet for the first hundred feet from the *street line* intersection, provided that no actual *street wall* either on the Fifth Avenue or on the *narrow street* frontage shall exceed a height of 125 feet at the *street line*.

Below the minimum required *street wall* height, recesses are limited to not more than 10 feet in depth and the aggregate area of recesses between two and 10 feet in depth shall not exceed 30 percent of the area of the *street wall* below minimum *street wall* height. The aggregate area of all recesses shall not exceed 50 percent of the area of the *street wall*. For the area above the minimum required *street wall* height, recesses are not restricted.

Above a height of 125 feet, a *street wall* shall be set back not less than 10 feet from the *street line*.

81-84
Mandatory Regulations and Prohibitions
The following requirements listed in this Section shall apply to all *developments*, *enlargements*, *extensions* or changes of *use* within the Subdistrict.

(a) Pedestrian access to *uses*

No access from the Fifth Avenue *street line* or within 50 feet of the Fifth Avenue *street line* shall be permitted to lobbies for office, *residential* or *hotel uses* or to any new *use* not listed in Use Group F, except when the *zoning lot* is inaccessible from any other *street*, in which case the total amount of frontage occupied by lobby space or entrance space for such uses shall not exceed 40 feet or 25 percent of the *building's* total *street* frontage, whichever is less.

No urban plaza or any part thereof shall be permitted on or within 50 feet of the Fifth Avenue *street line*.

(b) Off-street parking regulations

No off-street parking facilities are permitted within the Fifth Avenue Subdistrict.

(c) Off-street loading regulations

In no event shall access to *accessory* off-street loading berths be permitted on or within 50 feet of the Fifth

Avenue *street line*. Beyond 50 feet from the Fifth Avenue *street line*, for any *development* requiring three or more *accessory* loading berths, such berths shall be located below *street* grade. Access to such berths, however, shall be permitted at *street* grade.

Interior lots with a frontage only on Fifth Avenue or only on a *wide street* shall not contain loading berths.

Appendix D

San Francisco: Neighborhood Commercial Districts

The primary goal of the proposed neighborhood commercial rezoning is to achieve balanced growth for the neighborhood commercial districts of San Francisco—balance between different types of commercial uses, balance between residential and commercial uses, and balance between the neighborhood commercial districts and their surrounding neighborhoods. The primary innovation offered by the proposal is establishment of a single comprehensive zoning system for the approximately 210 neighborhood commercial areas in the city that fully recognizes the diversity that exists among these areas.

Current System

The neighborhood commercial districts consist of most commercial areas outside the Downtown area that are located among the residential neighborhoods of the city. They range from small groupings of 3 or 4 stores clustered around an intersection, to 3 and 4 block commercial strips to large diverse areas, such as North Beach. Existing zoning for these areas falls under a disparate assortment of classifications. Most fall under the C-1 (Neighborhood Shopping Districts) and the C-2 (Community Business Districts) zonings. Others fall under the RC (Residential Commercial Combined) zonings or the C-M (Heavy Commercial) zoning. By and large, the controls under these existing zonings are inadequate for main-

Source: San Francisco Department of City Planning, *Report on Neighborhood Commercial Rezoning*, 1987.

taining the delicate balance between diverse land use activities that historically have existed in most neighborhood commercial districts. In recent years, commercial growth in various district[s] has tipped this balance away from neighborhood-serving commercial uses and housing and more toward commercial uses that cater to a market beyond the immediate neighborhood or that have adverse impacts on adjacent residential livability.

Under the existing controls, many neighborhood commercial districts theoretically could become totally commercial in use and completely lose the mixed-use character which they have always shared. For example, the existing C-1 and C-2 zonings, under which most neighborhood commercial districts fall, permit a wide range of commercial uses at all floor levels as of right.

Proposed System

Under the proposed neighborhood commercial rezoning, this kind of full build-out of commercial activity is not possible. The proposed rezoning establishes a zoning system for the neighborhood commercial districts that gives thorough attention to the fine-grained mixture of uses which exist in these areas and provides a means of accommodating both commercial and residential growth in a more balanced and evolutionary manner.

It also provides a wider range of controls for dealing with the complexities of physical development and land use activity in neighborhood commercial areas. Some of these controls cover the same zoning categories as the existing zoning. Others are new. When the proposed controls cover the same zoning categories as the existing controls, they do so on a more individualized district-by-district basis so as to be more compatible with the particular characteristics of a given district. Reduced height limits are imposed in certain districts to assure that the scale of future development conforms to what already exists in these districts.

Greater attention is also given to the types of use permitted by floor, with limitations placed on converting existing upper-story residential space to commercial uses. The new controls provided by the proposed rezoning cover such things as lot size, use size, hours of commercial operation, etc., all of which are designed to reduce the scale and intensity of new commercial growth without necessarily discouraging growth itself. Their intent is to achieve greater compatibility between neighborhood commercial districts and their surrounding residential areas.

The proposed controls also have new provisions relating to the size, number, and locations of business signs and billboards. The controls provide for the continuation of legally established businesses which would not conform to the new controls. Such uses, called nonconforming uses, are permitted to continue in their current form, without further City authorization. Procedures for modifications, expansions, or relocation of such uses are included in the proposal controls.

What follows below are highlights of the neighborhood commercial rezoning proposal, including the Master Plan policies, the framework for implementing the zoning system, and a description of each of the proposed neighborhood commercial use districts.

Master Plan Policies

In conjunction with development of the proposed neighborhood commercial zoning controls, each element of the Master Plan was carefully reviewed and, if appropriate, updated, revised, or expanded to provide a relevant set of overall policy goals and objectives for the rezoning. The Master Plan objective most relevant to the neighborhood commercial areas of the city is Objective 8 of The Commerce and Industry Element which states, "maintain and strengthen viable neighborhood commercial areas easily accessible to residents." This objective has been thoroughly revised and proposed rezoning would have 9 policies as compared to the 5 which it currently contains. The proposed revisions cover new areas relating to urban design, historic and architectural preservation, and traffic and parking. They also provide specific guidelines for these new areas as well as for land use and residential conversions and demolition to assist the Planning Commission in its review of permit applications. The proposed Master Plan policies which establish the basis for the proposed rezoning are:

- Ensure and encourage the retention and provision of neighborhood-serving goods and services in the city's neighborhood commercial districts, while recognizing and encouraging diversity among the districts.
- Preserve and promote the mixed commercial-residential character in neighborhood commercial districts. Strike a balance between the preservation of existing affordable housing and needed expansion of commercial activity.
- Encourage the location of neighborhood shopping areas throughout the city so that essential retail goods and services are accessible to all residents.
- Discourage the creation of major new commercial areas except in conjunction with new supportive residential development and transportation capacity.
- Adopt specific zoning districts which conform to a generalized neighborhood commercial land use plan.
- Promote high quality urban design on commercial streets.
- Preserve historically or architecturally important buildings or groups of buildings in neighborhood commercial districts.
- Regulate uses so that traffic impacts and parking problems are minimized.
- Promote neighborhood commercial revitalization, including community-based and other economic development efforts where feasible.

Zoning Framework

To implement the above policies, a new article is proposed for the City Planning Code: Article 7—Neighborhood Commercial Districts. This article would establish the proposed neighborhood commercial zoning system. It sets forth the following general neighborhood commercial districts to cover most of the approximately 210 neighborhood commercial areas in the city:

NC-1 Neighborhood Commercial Cluster District
NC-2 Small-Scale Neighborhood Commercial District
NC-3 Moderate-Scale Neighborhood Commercial District
NC-S Neighborhood Shopping Center District

It also sets forth individual neighborhood commercial districts to cover 16 of the more intensely active commercial areas in the city:

Broadway	North Beach
Castro Street	Polk Street
Inner Clement Street	Sacramento Street
Outer Clement Street	Union Street
Upper Fillmore Street	Valencia Street
Haight Street	24th St.-Mission
Hayes-Gough	24th St.-Noe Valley
Upper Market Street	West Portal Avenue

A full range of controls is established to meet conditions unique to each of these districts. The controls for each district would be applicable to all property and uses in the district. Within the text of Article 7, a description and purpose statement for each district is accompanied by a chart which displays all applicable zoning controls either directly or by reference to other sections of the Code.

Appendix E

List of Interviews

Name	Position	Date
Richard Allen	Planning Commissioner, San Francisco	6/1/87
Noreen Ambrose	Deputy City Attorney, San Francisco	6/1/87
Jonathan Barnett	Urban Designer, Author, Former Member, Mayor Lindsay's Urban Design Group, New York City	3/9/87
Kent Barwick	President, Municipal Art Society, New York City	7/14/88 3/28/90
Joanna Battaglia	Former Member, Community Board No. 6, New York City	11/24/87
Bruce Bauman	Developer's Consultant, San Francisco	6/3/87
Bruce Bonacker	Neighborhood Association President, San Francisco	6/2/87
Bonnie Brauer	Executive Director, Association of Neighborhood Housing, New York City	3/12/87
Doris Deither	Former Member, Community Board No. 2, New York City	7/13/88
Donna Ducharme	Chicago Leeds Council	3/88-3/89 various dates
Donald Elliott	Former Chairman, New York City Planning Commission	3/13/87

Name	Position	Date
Edith Fischer	Officer, William Zeckendorf & Co., Former Chairwoman, Community Board No. 8, New York City	11/23/87
Martin Gallent	Zoning Attorney, Former Vice-Chairman, New York City Planning Commission	7/13/88
Alex Garvin	Developer, Former Staff Member, New York City Planning Commission	3/12/87
Howard Goldman	Zoning Attorney, New York City	7/12/88
Sandy Hornick	Planner, Current Director, Zoning Study Group, New York City Planning Commission	3/10/87 11/27/89
Inge Horton	San Francisco Department of City Planning	6/1/87 3/18/90
Conn Howe	Executive Director, New York City Planning Commission Staff	3/10/87
Robin Jones	San Francisco Department of City Planning	6/1/87
Michael Kwartler	Planner, Professor, Columbia University School of Planning, Former Staff Member, New York City Planning Commission	3/11/87
Jean Lerman	New York State Division of Housing	11/25/87
Bruce Lilienthal	Mayor's Small Business Advisory Commission, San Francisco	6/3/87
Gregory Longhini	Chicago Department of City Planning	3/22/90
Norman Marcus	Former General Counsel, New York City Planning Commission	3/9/87 4/28/87
Arthur Margon	Executive Director, Real Estate Board of New York City	7/22/88

Name	Position	Date
Victor Marrero	Attorney, Former Chairman, New York City Planning Commission	11/25/87
Harry O'Brien	Attorney, San Francisco	6/3/87
Michael Parley	Planner, Former Staff Member, New York City Planning Commission, Urban Study Group	3/9/87
Terry Pimsleur	Mayor's Small Business Advisory Commission, San Francisco	6/2/87
Raquel Ramati	Urban Designer, Former Member, Urban Design Group of New York City	3/12/87
Richard Rosan	Former President, New York Real Estate Board	11/23/87
Joseph Rose	Director, Community Board No. 5, New York City	4/27/87
William Ryan	Director, Community Board No. 4, New York City	4/28/87
Richard Satkin	New York City Planning Commission	11/27/89
Jeffrey Schanback	Former Assistant Corporation Counsel, New York City	7/11/88
Gerald Schoenfeld	Chairman, Shubert Theaters, Inc.	3/13/87
Brian Sullivan	Professor, Pratt University, Consultant to Clinton Association	3/13/87
Ronald Tom	CTA Architects, San Francisco	6/2/87
Patrick Too	Planner, Member, New York City Planning Commission, Mid-Manhattan Staff	3/10/87
Virginia Waters	Assistant Corporation Counsel, New York City	7/11/88 11/27/89
George Williams	San Francisco Department of City Planning	5/3/88

Name	Position	Date
Jane Winslow	North Beach Neighborhood Resident, San Francisco	6/1/87
Bernd Zimmerman	Director, Bronx Division, New York City Planning Commission	7/12/88
John E. Zuccotti	Attorney, Former Deputy Mayor, New York City, Former Chairman, New York City Planning Commission	3/11/87

About the Authors

Richard F. Babcock

Richard F. Babcock, one of the country's premier specialists in land use law, is a retired partner in the Chicago law firm of Ross and Hardies, where he spent 35 years representing public agencies, private developers, and builders. Since 1981, he has been Visiting Professor of Law at Duke University, Santa Clara University, Dartmouth College, University of Michigan, and Northern Illinois University. He also acts as a consultant to private developers and to cities and states throughout the country. Mr. Babcock is a former president of the American Planning Association and has served on many commissions and task forces. He has lectured throughout the United States and in Australia, and is the author or co-author of five books on land use law, including *The Zoning Game, City Zoning: The Once and Future Frontier*, and *The Zoning Game Revisited*, as well as dozens of articles.

Wendy U. Larsen

Wendy U. Larsen, a nationally known specialist in land use planning law, is a partner in the Chicago law firm of Siemon, Larsen & Purdy, which has additional offices in Boca Raton, Florida and Irvine, California. She is former chairman of the Planning and Law Division of the American Planning Association, the co-author of "Vested Rights: Balancing Public and Private Development Expectations," and the author of numerous other articles relating to land use issues. Ms. Larsen has represented both public and private sectors in land use matters, including environmental issues, impact fees, land development codes, and land use litigation.